Human Values and Ethics

A STEP TO SPIRITUAL LIFE

Dr. Geeta Devi

Human Values and Ethics: A step to Spiritual life

Dr. Geeta Devi

Human Values & Ethics: A step to Spiritual Life

About the Book

The book "Human Values and Ethics: A step to Spiritual Life" explores the profound connection between human values, ethics, and spirituality. It aims to guide readers through the complexities of living a value-driven life in today's fast-paced world. This book offers a unique perspective on how embracing ethical principles can lead to spiritual growth and fulfillment. In an era marked by rapid change and moral ambiguity, understanding and applying core human values is more important than ever. The chapters included in this book present both foundational and advanced insights from scholars and practitioners across various disciplines such as philosophy, psychology, and religious studies. By examining these diverse perspectives, readers will gain a deeper understanding of the essential role values and ethics play in leading a spiritually enriched life.

About The Editor

Dr. Geeta Devi is an Assistant Professor of Management at Maharaja Agraen School of Management, Maharaja Agrasen University, Baddi, Himachal Pradesh. She has accrued five years of experience in teaching, administration, and research. She holds an MBA, M.Com, UGC NET qualification in Management, HP SET qualification in Commerce and a Ph.D. in Management. Her primary areas of interest are Marketing and Human Resources. She has actively participated in various national and international conferences, contributing her expertise and research findings. She has published numerous research papers in reputable national and international journals, edited books, and conference proceedings.

Foreword

In an era marked by rapid technological advancements and shifting societal norms, the significance of human values and ethics has never been more profound. "Human Values and Ethics: A step to Spiritual Life" delves into the timeless principles that underpin ethical behavior and spiritual fulfillment, offering readers a roadmap to navigate the complexities of modern life with integrity and purpose.

This book is a testament to the enduring relevance of human values and ethics in fostering a spiritually enriched life. It explores diverse perspectives from philosophy, psychology, and religious studies, providing readers with a comprehensive understanding of how ethical living can lead to personal and collective well-being. Through thoughtful reflection and practical guidance, "Human Values and Ethics: A Lead to Spiritual Life" invites readers to embark on a journey of self-discovery and spiritual growth.

As we navigate the challenges and opportunities of contemporary life, this book serves as a beacon, reminding us of the importance of living with authenticity, compassion, and moral clarity.

Dr. Geeta Devi
MBA, M.Com, Ph.D (Management)
Assistant Professor
Department of Management
Maharaja Agrasen Unversity,
Baddi, Solan, Himachal Pradesh

DEDICATION

I, Dr. Geeta Devi, with the blessings of the Almighty, my grandparents, and my family, have written my first book. I dedicate this work to my father, late Sh. Bhupinder Singh, and my grandfather, late Sh. Deep Ram.

The inspiration for writing this book comes from the Holy Book, "The Bhagwat Gita," which reveals the reality of the existence of everything in this Universe. I hope this book will guide its readers towards leading a spiritual life.

Dr. Geeta Devi

ACKNOWLEDGEMENT

With the blessings of the Almighty, my grandparents, and my family, I am deeply honored to present my first book, *Human Values and Ethics: A Step to Spiritual Life.* I dedicate this work to the cherished memory of my father, the late Sh. Bhupinder Singh, and my grandfather, the late Sh. Deep Ram.

I extend my heartfelt gratitude to the Honorable Vice-Chancellor of Maharaja Agrasen University, Professor R.K. Gupta, Chancellor Nominee Mr. Suresh Gupta, and the Director of the Department of Management, Prof. Dr. A.K. Vashisht, for their unwavering encouragement and blessings throughout the writing process.

I am profoundly indebted to the numerous authors, writers, and researchers whose works have provided me with invaluable knowledge and insight. Their contributions, though indirect, have been instrumental in shaping the concepts within this book. I believe that their collective wisdom will greatly benefit readers, guiding them towards a life enriched with spirituality, ethics, and nobility.

Preface

In a world where the pace of life is ever-accelerating and the lines between right and wrong often blur, the importance of grounding oneself in human values and ethics cannot be overstated. This book, "Human Values and Ethics: A Lead to Spiritual Life," seeks to illuminate the path towards a life enriched by spiritual fulfillment through the understanding and application of timeless principles.

This work begins with an exploration of values, delving into their meaning, significance, and various types. By understanding the foundational values that shape human behavior, readers can appreciate their role in fostering personal and societal well-being.

Next, we delve into the realm of ethics, discussing its principles and various approaches. Ethical frameworks provide a compass for navigating complex moral landscapes, and this section aims to equip readers with the tools to make sound ethical decisions.

The book also addresses morality through the lens of Kohlberg's Theory of Moral Development, offering insights into the stages of moral reasoning and growth. This theoretical foundation is complemented by a discussion on Dharma and the Four Purusharthas, illustrating the Indian philosophical perspective on the aims of human life.

Karma and Swadharma are examined, emphasizing the significance of action and personal duty in the pursuit of a meaningful life. The concept of Panchkoshas, or the five layers of human existence, is introduced, providing a holistic view of the human experience.

The exploration continues with the Three Gunas and Four Ashramas, which offer a framework for understanding human nature and the stages of life in Indian philosophy. The Nyaya Theory of Knowledge and the Four Pramanas further enrich this discourse by presenting a classical approach to epistemology and the validation of knowledge.

Spirituality is introduced as a vital aspect of human existence, with an exploration of the spiritual laws that govern the universe. This section aims to bridge the gap between ethical living and spiritual growth, highlighting the interconnectedness of these realms.

Finally, the book addresses the practical applications of these principles through an introduction to yoga and meditation for stress management. These practices are presented as tools for achieving inner peace and aligning one's life with higher spiritual ideals.

It is my hope that this book will serve as a guide for readers seeking to navigate the complexities of modern life with integrity, compassion, and spiritual insight. By embracing the principles outlined in these pages, may you find a path to a more fulfilling and spiritually enriched life.

Dr. Geeta Devi

10

Chapter 1

THE ESSENCE OF VALUES

Introduction

The term "value" is broad and encompasses various meanings, such as importance, magnitude, worth, and significance. Value refers to something related to a person's relationship with their goals. Values are learned through observation and understanding of one's surroundings, including family, friends, culture, and religion. They help us determine what is important in our lives and guide our actions, attitudes, and motives.

Meaning

A person's values reveal their beliefs about:

- What is good or bad,

- What is right or wrong, and

- What is desirable or undesirable?

In essence, values serve as the motives or the basis for choosing between different courses of action, especially when making critical decisions. High values lead to objective, fair outcomes and ensure the welfare of those involved, while low values do the opposite. Values also reflect the personal qualities we aspire to embody, including:

- The type of person we want to become,

- How we treat ourselves and others,

- How we interact with the world.

Definitions

According to Swami Vivekananda, "Value is the principle of action or guiding principle that is respected, desirable, and important in the particular society in which the person lives."

Milton Rokeach defines values as "global beliefs that guide actions and judgments across a variety of situations."

Values are the driving forces behind purposeful actions. They influence an individual's perception of problems and the decisions made to address them. While values vary from person to person, they are integral to understanding and shaping our identity and character. They help us realize that "what we are is more important than what we have" and provide a sense of relief and contentment that is unparalleled.

Importance of Values

Values are crucial for several reasons:

- They help individuals become responsible citizens.

- Moral values taught by parents aid children in distinguishing right from wrong.

- Values contribute to building a strong character.

- They help reduce violence, corruption, dishonesty, and other social issues.

- Values counteract negative influences in society.

- They guide moral conduct in our lives.

- Values direct our behavior and give purpose to our lives.

- They are essential for personal and societal development.

- Values play a key role in shaping a person's thoughts, actions, emotions, and reasoning.

- They help us appreciate that our identity is more important than material possessions.

The Role of Moral Values in Building a Nation

Our civilization is currently undergoing rapid changes, leading to increased incidents of anti-social behavior, immorality, and corruption. This decline in moral values is noticeable at various levels, including schools and universities. Swami Vivekananda emphasized the importance of education in cultivating morality, honesty, and good character. According to him, schools are crucial in shaping the future of our nation by imparting values such as love, respect, honesty, and patriotism.

Character formation requires hard work and the development of moral and spiritual values. The ancient Indian education system, which presented high ideals to students, serves as a model for today's education. Educators should inspire students with strong values, as an education system devoid of character is incomplete.

Religions also contribute to our values. While the specific elements of different religions may vary, respect for all religions and love for all beings are universal goals.

Sources of Values

Values are developed through various sources:

Familial Factors: The family plays a crucial role in socializing individuals by teaching values through rewards and punishments.

Societal Factors: Schools significantly influence value development through discipline and interactions with teachers and peers.

Personal Factors: Individual traits such as intelligence, education, and personal experiences shape one's values.

Religions, economic systems, and political institutions also impact the formation of values. Values can be categorized into:

- **Terminal Values:** These are ends to be achieved, such as a comfortable life, self-respect, and wisdom.

- **Instrumental Values:** These are means to achieve desired ends, such as ambition, honesty, and independence.

Terminal Values ("ends") Instrumental Values ("means")

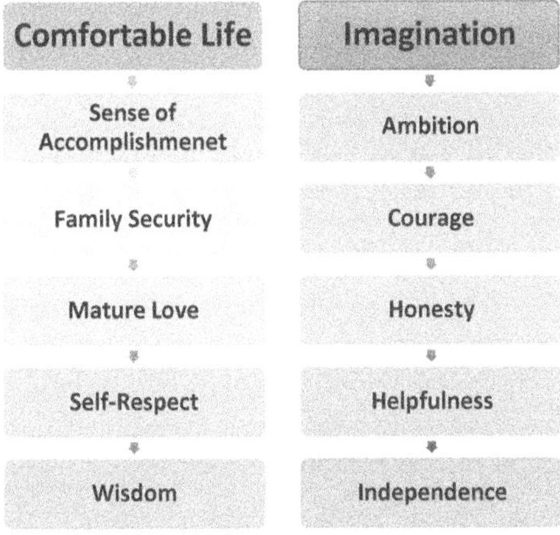

Fig. 1 Terminal and Instrumental Values

Types of Values

According to Allport, values can be classified into six categories based on orientation:

- **Theoretical:** Interest in discovering truth through reasoning and systematic thinking.

- **Economic:** Focus on practicality and accumulation of wealth.

- **Aesthetic:** Appreciation for beauty and artistic harmony.

- **Social:** Concern for human relationships and affection.

- **Political:** Interest in gaining and using power to influence others.

- **Religious:** Emphasis on unity and spiritual values.

Each person may prioritize these values differently based on their understanding and behavior. Virtue ethics emphasizes that practicing virtues leads to excellence of character. Intrinsic values (e.g., honesty) are valued for their own sake, while extrinsic values (e.g., wealth) are valued for their outcomes.

Basic Ethical Values

Basic ethical values are rooted in the sanctity of human dignity and include:

- **Autonomy:** The right to make decisions, worship, and express oneself freely.

- **Justice:** Fair treatment and equal rights.

Moral Values

Moral values are essential for a fulfilling life and include both individual and social values:

- **Individual Values:** Love, friendship, selfresponsibility, and autonomy.

- **Social Values:** Unity, collective responsibility, and fairness.

Commercial Values

Commercial values pertain to market activities and include aspects such as the free market, earning capacity, property rights, and contract autonomy.

Conclusion

Human values form the foundation for a cohesive society, bridging individual and social dimensions. They help us discern right from wrong and good from bad. Families, groups, and societies share common values, with the family being a fundamental unit of social organization. Emphasizing value-based education from school to university levels is crucial for preserving and protecting human values. If youth can set a positive example, it will benefit both current and future generations.

Chapter 2

FOUNDATIONS OF ETHICS: PRINCIPLES AND APPROACHES

Introduction

The term "ethics" is derived from the Greek word "ethos," meaning character. Ethics refers to the ideals and principles that guide an individual's behavior, motivating them to act with honesty and integrity. When evaluating actions from the perspective of public welfare, whether something is right or wrong, we are guided by ethics. While written laws govern official matters, ethics serve as a self-regulating system that maintains a balance between individual interests and societal good, particularly when legal oversight is lacking. Mahatma Gandhi believed that while human beings may never achieve divine perfection, they should strive to embody virtues such as truth, love, non-violence, tolerance, fearlessness, charity, and service to humanity.

Meaning

Ethics is a branch of philosophy focused on studying ideal human behavior and ways of being. It systematically examines and differentiates between right and wrong, good and bad, and admirable and deplorable behaviors concerning the well-being and relationships among sentient beings. Swami Vivekananda emphasized that a nation's greatness is determined not by its laws but by the virtue of its people. Ethics helps individuals become good citizens by distinguishing between moral and immoral actions, with moral actions being those that are unselfish.

Definitions

- **Larry Churchill:** "Ethics, understood as the capacity to think critically about moral values and direct our actions in terms of such values, is a generic human capacity."

- **Richard William, Paul, and Linda Elder:** "A set of concepts and principles that guide us in determining what behavior helps or harms sentient creatures."

- **Swami Vivekananda:** "Ethics is nothing but a code of conduct that helps a man to be a good citizen."

- **Cambridge Dictionary of Philosophy:** "The word ethics is commonly used interchangeably with 'morality' to mean… and sometimes it is used more narrowly to mean the moral principles of a particular tradition, group, or individual."

Areas of Study

Ethics can be divided into four major areas of study:

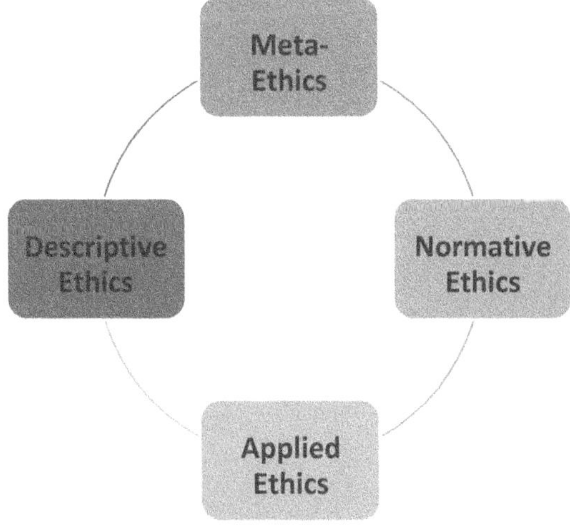

Fig. 2 Types of Ethics

1. **Meta-Ethics:** Examines the theoretical meaning and reference of moral propositions and how their truth values are determined, such as concepts like good, happiness, and virtuous character.

2. **Normative Ethics:** Focuses on determining moral courses of action and what individuals should do in various situations, including what type of character one should strive for.

3. **Applied Ethics:** Uses ethical theory to address specific moral issues in various domains of action.

4. **Descriptive Ethics:** Studies what people think about morality and how they actually behave, focusing on descriptive aspects of morals.

Ethical Views

Ethical thinking often falls along a continuum between two contrasting views:

- **Relativist View:** Judgments about right and wrong are based on cultural and situational contexts. This view includes:

    o **Ethical Subjectivism:** Belief that individuals create their own morality, and there are no objective moral truths—only personal opinions.

o **Cultural Relativism:** Moral evaluations are rooted in and cannot be separated from the experiences, beliefs, and behaviors of a particular culture. Thus, what is considered wrong in one culture may not be in another.

- **Universalist View:** Belief that there are universal or objective moral principles that should be applied regardless of cultural or situational differences.

Approaches to Ethical Standards

Here are five approaches to ethical standards:

1. **The Utilitarian Approach:** An ethical action is one that produces the greatest balance of good over harm. It focuses on consequences and aims to maximize overall good and minimize harm.

2. **The Rights Approach:** Ethical actions are those that protect and respect the moral rights of those affected, emphasizing human dignity and the right to be treated as ends in themselves.

3. **The Justice Approach:** Based on the idea that all people should be treated equally or fairly, this approach assesses actions according to principles of fairness and impartiality, such as equitable remuneration for work.

4. **The Common Good Approach:** This approach emphasizes the importance of social relationships and the welfare of all members of society. Ethical actions are those that respect and promote the well-being of the community, including systems like laws, healthcare, and emergency services.

5. **The Virtue Approach:** Ethical actions are those consistent with ideal virtues that support the full development of humanity, such as honesty, courage, compassion, and fairness.

Fundamental Ethical Principles

The four fundamental ethical principles are:

1. **The Principle of Respect for Autonomy:** Every individual has the right to make their own decisions concerning their life. This principle emphasizes selfrule and the dignity of individual choices.

2. **The Principle of Beneficence:** We are obligated to perform actions that benefit others and promote happiness. This principle advocates for creating more good than harm in the world.

3. **The Principle of Non-Maleficence:** We should avoid causing harm to others and minimize harm when it cannot be avoided. This principle underscores the importance of protecting well-being and providing care.

4. **The Principle of Justice:** All individuals should be treated equally and fairly, without bias related to religion, race, color, caste, or gender. This principle ensures that people receive what they deserve in an equitable manner.

Professional Ethics

Professional ethics pertains to the conduct expected from professionals within their workplaces. It includes:

- **Code of Ethics:** A set of norms that define the core purpose of a profession, outlining ethical principles and standards of practice.

- **Code of Conduct:** Specific rules or norms related to professional behavior, including fairness, integrity, and honesty, applicable to professions such as law, medicine, and accounting.

Social Ethics

Social ethics refers to the principles that govern how members of a society deal with issues such as justice, fairness, poverty, and individual rights. It varies across cultures and countries, reflecting the norms and values of different societies. Individuals have a responsibility to respect and follow societal norms and laws while balancing individual autonomy with justice and the common good.

Business Ethics

Business ethics involves managing responsibilities towards all parties related to a business, including shareholders, employees, customers, suppliers, and the public. According to W.O. Wheeler, "Business ethics is an art and science of maintaining a proper harmonious relationship with society and recognizing the moral responsibility for the rightness and wrongness of business practices." Ethical business conduct should be characterized by honesty and trustworthiness.

Conclusion

Understanding and applying ethics in our daily lives is crucial for distinguishing between good and bad, right and wrong, and making righteous decisions. Ethics provides a framework for evaluating our actions and their impact on others, guiding us towards a more just and harmonious society.

Chapter 3

ETHICAL THEORIES AND MORAL PRINICPLES

Introduction

Ethical theories provide systematic and coherent frameworks for thinking about moral issues, guiding individuals in making ethical decisions and understanding the principles that underpin moral judgments. These theories offer diverse perspectives, ranging from rule-based approaches to those emphasizing the consequences of actions or the character of the moral agent.

1. Deontological Ethics

Deontological ethics, primarily associated with Immanuel Kant, is an ethical theory that emphasizes duties and rules. According to this view, actions are morally right or wrong based on their adherence to specific rules or principles, regardless of the consequences.

- **Key Concepts**:

    o **Duty**: Actions are morally obligatory if they align with a set of duties.

    o **Categorical Imperative**: Kant's principle that one should act only according to maxims that can be universally applied.

    o **Moral Law**: A set of universal rules that are inherent and must be followed.

- **Strengths**:

  - Provides clear guidelines for moral behavior.

  - Emphasizes the importance of intention and principle.

- **Weaknesses**:

  - Can be rigid and inflexible.

  - May lead to conflicting duties with no clear resolution.

2. Utilitarianism

Utilitarianism, developed by philosophers such as Jeremy Bentham and John Stuart Mill, is a consequentialist theory that judges the morality of actions based on their outcomes. The central tenet is that the best action is the one that maximizes overall happiness or pleasure and minimizes pain.

- **Key Concepts**:

  - **Greatest Happiness Principle**: Actions are right if they promote the greatest happiness for the greatest number of people.

  - **Utility**: The measure of the balance of pleasure over pain.

- **Strengths**:

  - Focuses on the consequences of actions, making it practical and outcome-oriented.

  - Encourages actions that benefit the majority.

- **Weaknesses**:

    o Can justify actions that are intuitively immoral if they result in greater overall happiness.

    o Difficult to accurately measure and compare the consequences of different actions.

3. Virtue Ethics

Virtue ethics, rooted in the philosophy of Aristotle, emphasizes the character and virtues of the moral agent rather than specific actions or consequences. This theory focuses on the development of moral character and the cultivation of virtues such as courage, temperance, and wisdom.

- **Key Concepts**:

    o **Virtue**: A trait or quality deemed morally good.

    o **Eudaimonia**: Often translated as "flourishing" or "well-being," it is the highest human good.

- **Strengths**:

    o Encourages holistic personal development and moral growth.

    o Flexible and context-sensitive.

- **Weaknesses**:

    o Lacks clear guidelines for action in specific situations.

- o The concept of virtue can be culturally relative and subjective.

4. Ethical Relativism

Ethical relativism posits that morality is not universal and that moral standards are culturally or individually determined. According to this view, what is considered morally right or wrong varies from one society to another or from one individual to another.

- **Key Concepts**:

  - o **Cultural Relativism**: Moral standards are defined by cultural beliefs and practices.

  - o **Subjectivism**: Moral judgments are based on individual preferences and perspectives.

- **Strengths**:

  - o Promotes tolerance and understanding of diverse moral perspectives.

  - o Recognizes the influence of cultural and personal contexts on moral judgments.

- **Weaknesses**:

  - o Can lead to moral paralysis, where no action can be deemed objectively wrong.

  - o Challenges the notion of universal human rights and ethical standards.

5. Social Contract Theory

Social contract theory, associated with philosophers like Thomas Hobbes, John Locke, and Jean-Jacques Rousseau, suggests that moral and political obligations are based on a contract or agreement among individuals to form a society. This theory posits that individuals consent, either explicitly or implicitly, to surrender some of their freedoms in exchange for security and social order.

- **Key Concepts**:

    o **State of Nature**: A hypothetical condition where there are no social structures or rules.

    o **Social Contract**: An agreement among individuals to form a society and abide by its rules.

- **Strengths**:

    o Provides a foundation for the legitimacy of political authority and laws.

    o Emphasizes the role of mutual agreement and consent in forming moral standards.

- **Weaknesses**:

    o Assumes a hypothetical situation that may not reflect real human conditions.

    o Can be interpreted in ways that justify oppressive social structures.

Conclusion

Understanding these ethical theories provides a comprehensive framework for analyzing moral issues and making ethical decisions. Each theory offers unique insights and challenges, reflecting the complexity and diversity of moral philosophy. By examining these theories, individuals can develop a nuanced approach to ethics, incorporating principles from various perspectives to navigate the moral landscape of their personal and professional lives.

Chapter 4

Morality: Kohlberg's Theory of Moral Development

Introduction

Morality refers to the dimension of assessing actions, involving practical judgment, and interpreting their significance. It is a mode of vision that connects to societal norms and legal practices. The morality of a society is related to its mores—the customs accepted by a group as right or wrong—as well as to the laws that impose legal prohibitions and sanctions on activities considered immoral. Morality can thus be defined as the customary, sociolegal practices and activities deemed significantly right or wrong, the rules governing those activities, and the values embedded in and fostered by these practices.

Morality is used in two broad senses:

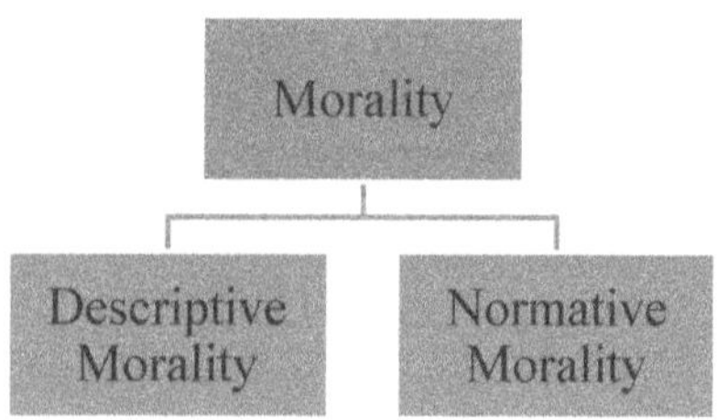

Fig. 3 Types of Morality

- **Descriptive Morality:** Refers to the specific code of conduct set by a society, group, or individual, such as those defined by religious or cultural norms.

- **Normative Morality:** Refers to a code of conduct that all rational persons would agree upon under specified conditions.

Major Features of Morality

Morality's features fall into two categories:

- **Formal Features:** These include prescriptivity, universalizability, overridingness, non-authority dependence, and being about objective facts. Formal features specify the normative character of moral judgments.

- **Material Features:** These focus on benefits and harms, specifying the content of moral judgments, such as the attitudes and conduct prescribed by moral principles.

Kohlberg's Theory of Moral Development

Lawrence Kohlberg's theory of moral development, which builds upon Jean Piaget's earlier work, describes how children develop moral reasoning. Kohlberg identified six stages of moral development, grouped into three levels: preconventional, conventional, and post-conventional morality. His research, including the use of dilemmas like the Heinz dilemma, explores how individuals justify their actions in various moral situations.

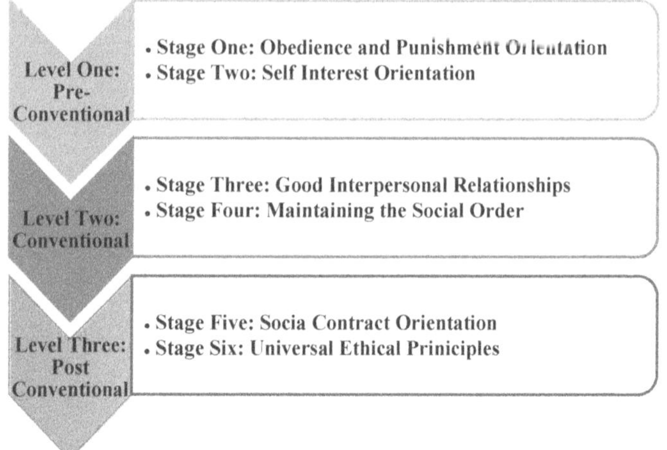

Fig. 4 Kohlberg's Theory of Moral Development

Level One: Pre-Conventional

Stage One: Obedience and Punishment Orientation This stage focuses on the direct consequences of actions. Behavior is judged based on whether it results in punishment. For example, a child learns not to lie to avoid getting spanked.

Stage Two: Self Interest Orientation This stage is driven by self-interest, with actions evaluated based on personal gain. For instance, a child might help with chores if promised a reward, like a chocolate.

Level Two: Conventional

Stage Three: Good Interpersonal Relationships At this stage, individuals seek to be "good" by conforming to societal norms and maintaining good relationships. Actions are judged by their impact on interpersonal relationships and the desire to be liked.

Stage Four: Maintaining the Social Order Here, individuals adhere to laws and societal rules to maintain social order. Respect for authority and the rule of law become central, with adherence to laws viewed as crucial for societal functioning.

Level Three: Post-Conventional

Stage Five: Social Contract Orientation This stage recognizes the diversity of individual perspectives and the need for mutual respect. It advocates for rules that promote the general welfare and allows for change if they do not benefit the majority.

Stage Six: Universal Ethical Principles

At this stage, individuals act based on universal ethical principles, such as justice and human rights, regardless of legal or societal constraints. Moral laws are self-chosen, and this stage is reached by very few individuals.

Conclusion

Morality guides us in discerning the rightness or wrongness of our actions. It indicates what is good or bad, right or wrong, just or unjust, and outlines ethical behavior. Morality is often used interchangeably with ethics, but they are distinct concepts. Ethics helps us understand what is right or wrong, whereas morality refers to the practice of making decisions based on those understandings. Morality guides behavior according to societal norms or values, while ethics provides a broader framework for evaluating these norms. Morality often stems from religious or cultural beliefs, but it is a guide to conduct aimed at preventing harm to others.

broader framework for evaluating these norms. Morality often stems from religious or cultural beliefs, but it is a guide to conduct aimed at preventing harm to others.

Chapter 5

Dharma and Life's Aims: An Introduction to the Four Purusharthas

Introduction

Purusharthas refers to the aims or goals of human life. The term is a combination of two Sanskrit words: *purus* (human being) and *artha* (goal). These are the four proper goals of human life according to Hindu philosophy. They represent the inherent values that guide a fulfilling and meaningful existence.

While humans and animals share basic needs such as seeking food, rest, and self-protection, what differentiates humans is their intellectual capacity. Humans can reason, learn from past mistakes, and project future outcomes. This intellectual capacity allows for the pursuit of various goals, known as Purusharthas.

According to Hinduism, a person's life should aim to achieve the following four Purusharthas:

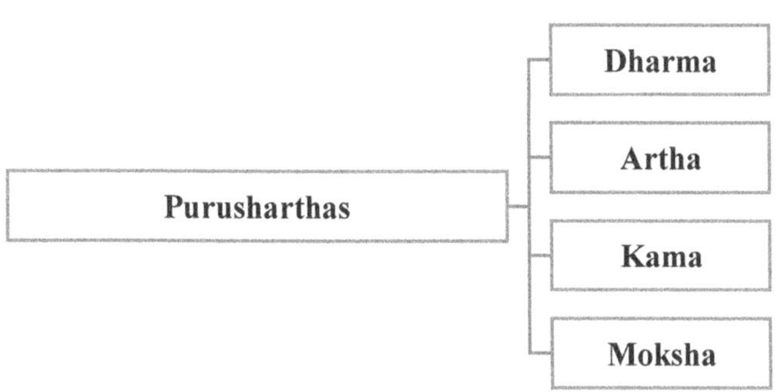

Fig. 5 Types of Purusharthas

1. Dharma

Dharma is a fundamental concept in Indian philosophy, derived from the Sanskrit word *dhiri*, meaning to uphold or sustain. It can be translated as religion, law, order, duty, or ethics. Dharma is associated with responsibility, righteousness, and adherence to one's duty based on societal and personal circumstances.

- o **Meaning:** Dharma involves performing duties and responsibilities in accordance with one's stage and position in life. It is seen as conducive to the highest good, promoting orderliness, justice, social harmony, and personal fulfillment. Dharma is often linked to moral conduct and personal virtue. According to the Vedas, Dharma elevates an individual and helps attain the ultimate goals of life.

- o **Hindu and Buddhist Perspectives:** In Hinduism, Dharma is a code of conduct essential for leading a moral life. For Buddhists, it represents eternal truth and ultimate reality. The *Manu Smriti* states: "One should speak what is true, one should speak what is pleasant, one should not speak what is true if it is not pleasant, nor what is pleasant if it is false. This is the ancient Dharma."

- o **Bhishma's Definition:** In the *Mahabharata*, Bhishma describes Dharma as that which sustains and uplifts living beings, emphasizing harmony within oneself and with the surrounding environment.

2. Artha

Artha refers to the pursuit of material wealth and security. It encompasses the basic needs for survival, comfort, and some degree of luxury.

> o **Meaning:** Artha is about achieving material prosperity and security. It includes not only financial wealth but also knowledge, health, skills, and relationships. This goal helps individuals fulfill their needs and desires in a balanced and ethical manner.

3. Kama

Kama pertains to the pursuit of pleasure and enjoyment. This includes sensual pleasures but also extends to aesthetic, intellectual, and emotional experiences.

> o **Meaning:** Kama involves enjoying life's pleasures in a way that aligns with Dharma. It includes appreciating art, love, intimacy, and kindness. The goal is to experience pleasure in a manner that is virtuous and supportive of one's Dharma. Kama is often misunderstood as merely a guide to sensual pleasure, but it actually provides a framework for a well-rounded and pleasurable life.

4. Moksha

Moksha is the ultimate goal of liberation from the cycle of birth and death. It signifies freedom from all binding desires and attachments.

    ○ **Meaning:** Moksha represents the realization of self and freedom from worldly bonds. It is attained through self-discipline, knowledge, and the grace of a spiritual teacher. Moksha involves inner freedom, peace, and bliss. It is described as liberation from Maya (illusion) and the cycles of rebirth, leading to divine happiness and self-realization.

Conclusion

The four Purusharthas—Dharma, Artha, Kama, and Moksha—remain relevant and applicable across time. By pursuing these goals in a righteous manner and in accordance with Dharma, one can lead a successful, balanced, and fulfilling life.

Chapter 6

Karma and Swadharma: The Path of Duty and Action

Introduction

Karma refers to the actions we perform and the inevitable results that follow from them, whether in this life or in future reincarnations. It encompasses every form of action—thoughts, words, and deeds. Since action is an inherent part of existence, no one can remain inactive even for a moment. Actions arise from the natural laws of cause and effect. Positive actions yield positive results, while negative actions lead to negative outcomes. The idea of Karma can be likened to a balance sheet where deeds not settled in the present are carried over to future lives. Therefore, one's actions should be performed within the framework of Dharma.

Karma Yogi

A **Karma Yogi** is someone who is aware of their Atman (self) and remains engaged in action while understanding that, despite the activity of the intellect, mind, and senses, they are merely spectators. This person acts without attachment, maintaining purity and detachment, and surrenders to divine will. By removing desires, attachments, and ego, the Karma Yogi transcends rebirth.

Types of Karma

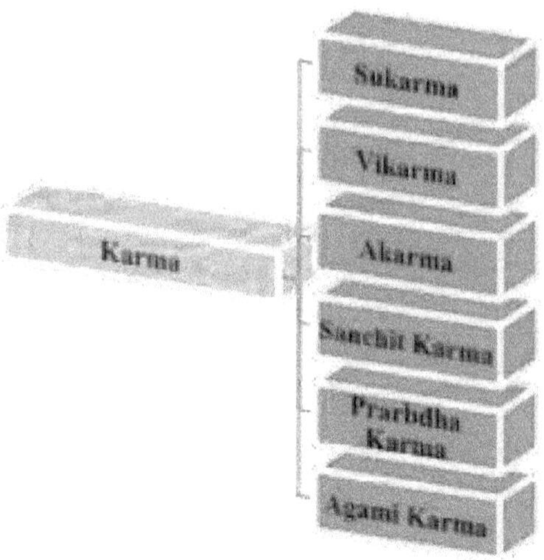

Fig. 6 Types of Karma

1. **Sukarma**: Refers to good deeds or actions performed for the welfare of others. These are actions that benefit humanity and align with moral values.

2. **Vikarma**: Denotes selfish actions that harm others or lead to lower life forms. These actions are driven by negative intent and result in adverse consequences.

3. **Akarma**: Actions performed without any material expectations or rewards, but simply to achieve inner happiness and please the divine. Akarma leads to liberation from the cycle of birth and death.

4. **Sanchit Karma**: The accumulated actions from past lives that are yet to bear fruit.

5. **Prarabdha Karma**: The actions currently in effect that influence the present life.

6. **Agami Karma**: The actions performed in the present that will impact future lives.

The Four Varnas

The social order is categorized into four Varnas, each corresponding to a specific duty:

1. **Brahmins (Priests)**: Serve through spirituality, embodying qualities like serenity, purity, and devotion.

2. **Kshatriyas (Warriors)**: Serve through heroism, possessing qualities such as bravery, leadership, and protection.

3. **Vaishyas (Merchants)**: Serve through skills related to trade, agriculture, and livestock care.

4. **Shudras (Servants)**: Serve by supporting the other three Varnas through service.

Following one's Varna aligns with Dharma and maintains societal harmony.

Nishkama Karma

Nishkama Karma involves performing actions without desire for personal gain. According to Lord Krishna, such actions are done selflessly, without attachment to the results. Performing one's duties in this manner, as an offering to the divine, ensures that actions align with Dharma, and the results are taken care of by divine will.

The belief that "everything happens for a reason" underscores the idea that our current experiences reflect our past actions and shape our future. By engaging in righteous actions and avoiding attachment to outcomes, one influences their destiny positively.

Concept of Swadharma

Swadharma combines two Sanskrit words: *swa* (self) and *Dharma* (lawful conduct). It represents the righteous conduct specific to an individual's nature and circumstances.

- **Swadharma in Practice**: Just as the sun, moon, and natural elements follow their own Dharma, humans must follow their own Swadharma. For example, in the *Bhagavad Gita*, Arjuna is guided by Lord Krishna to perform his duty as a warrior, reflecting his Swadharma.

- **Importance of Swadharma**: Acting according to one's nature—skills, talents, and personal disposition—is essential for personal growth. Swadharma involves performing actions that resonate with one's true self, even if imperfectly. Krishna emphasizes that fulfilling one's Swadharma is better than performing another's Dharma perfectly.

Conclusion

In essence, one's actions guided by their Swabhav (inner nature) align with Dharma. By adhering to Swadharma, individuals ensure they follow their true path and contribute positively to the greater good. Each person's journey involves discovering their Swadharma, which provides a path to live authentically and meaningfully.

Chapter 7

The Panchkoshas: Layers of Human Existence

Introduction

Panchkoshas is derived from two Sanskrit words: *Panch* meaning "five" and *Kosha* meaning "sheath." This concept from Indian traditions provides a framework for understanding the layers of consciousness and their relationship with the mind, life force, and body. According to Vedanta philosophy, our true self is enveloped by these five sheaths. The Taittiriya Upanishad describes human existence as layers, similar to an onion, ranging from coarse to fine. Each sheath corresponds to different aspects of our experience and mental processes, guiding us from the gross to the subtle levels of consciousness.

The Three Bodies

Human existence is framed by three bodies that encompass all the Panchkoshas:

1. **Gross Body (Sthula Sharira)**: The physical body.

2. **Subtle Body (Linga Sharira)**: The vital energy field.

3. **Causal Body (Karana Sharira)**: The ego.

The Panchkoshas model, detailed in the Taittiriya Upanishad, explores the five sheaths and their psychological manifestations.

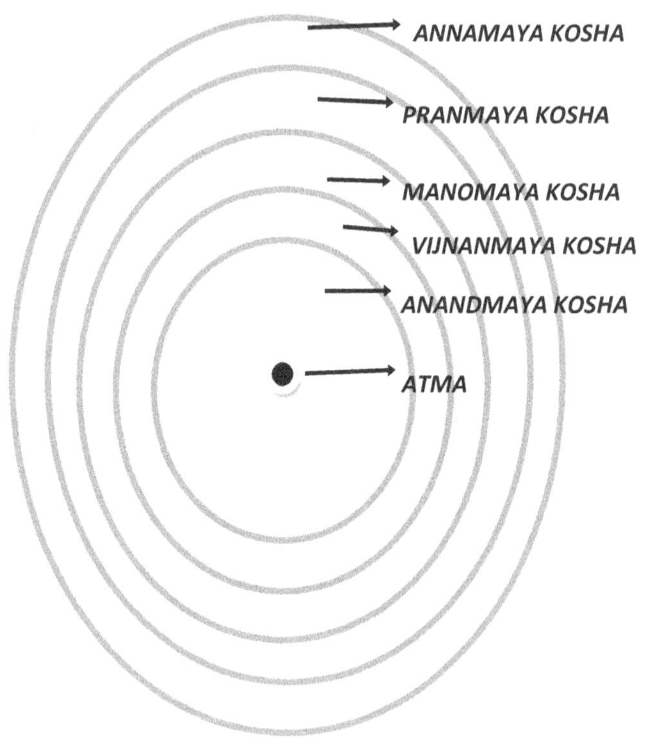

Fig.7 The Pancha Koshas: Level of Consciousness

The Five Sheaths

1. Annamaya Kosha

- o **Meaning**: Derived from *Anna*, meaning

"food", this is the outermost layer, known as the "food body."

- o **Characteristics**: This sheath is concerned with the physical body and its functions, such as birth, growth, and decay. It includes everything related to material existence and physical health.

- o **Functions**: Annamaya Kosha performs two primary functions—maintaining balance and health, and processing information. It emphasizes physical fitness and activities like sports and exercise.

2. Pranamaya Kosha

- o **Meaning**: Derived from *Prana*, meaning "life force", this is the second layer, known as the "vital force body."

- o **Characteristics**: This sheath is associated with the breath and vital energy that sustains life. It links the body and mind, influencing emotions and energy levels.

- o **Functions**: Pranamaya Kosha regulates the vital energy within the body, facilitating higher levels of consciousness, freedom, and vitality. It is linked to practices like meditation and physical exercise.

3. Manomaya Kosha

- o **Meaning**: Derived from *Manas*, meaning "mind", this is the third layer, known as the "mind body."

- o **Characteristics**: This sheath deals with emotions, thoughts, and perceptions. It processes sensory input and influences emotional states such as anger, joy, and sadness.

- o **Functions**: Manomaya Kosha is responsible for cognitive processes and creative thinking. It influences how we interact with the world through our emotions and perceptions.

4. Vijnanamaya Kosha

- o **Meaning**: Derived from *Vijnana*, meaning "knowledge", this is the fourth layer, known as the "intellectual body."

- o **Characteristics**: This sheath is associated with intellectual functions, including discrimination, decision-making, and wisdom. It integrates and applies knowledge to guide actions.

- o **Functions**: Vijnanamaya Kosha helps in discerning right from wrong and making informed decisions. It supports intellectual pursuits such as research, literature, and management.

5. Anandamaya Kosha

- o **Meaning**: Derived from *Ananda*, meaning "bliss", this is the innermost layer, known as the "bliss body."

- o **Characteristics**: This sheath is closest to the true self (Atman) and reflects inner joy and peace. It represents the state of pure happiness and contentment, independent of external circumstances.

- o **Functions**: Anandamaya Kosha provides a foundation of inner bliss and harmony. It is characterized by a profound sense of peace and joy, regardless of external events.

Conclusion

The Panchkoshas model helps in understanding the layers of consciousness and their impact on human experience. By delving into each sheath, individuals can gain insights into their true nature and achieve inner bliss. Reaching the Anandamaya Kosha allows one to experience profound happiness and tranquility, transcending material concerns and aligning with the true self.

Chapter 8

Three Gunas and Four Ashramas: Frameworks of Human Nature and Life Stages

Introduction

According to Lord Krishna, the cosmic nature is governed by three fundamental qualities known as **Gunas**. These Gunas are the basis of all creation and influence the individual soul's interaction with the world. Understanding these cosmic qualities is crucial for achieving success and happiness both in worldly and spiritual life. The term **Trigunas** combines two Sanskrit words: *Tri* (three) and *Guna* (qualities). Sankara's explanation of Guna Samkhyan, rooted in the system of Kapila, elaborates on these three Gunas and their impact on personality.

The Greek word *persona*, meaning "mask," reflects the concept of personality, indicating how individuals project themselves. In Indian philosophy, **Prakriti** denotes one's inherent nature, derived from *Pra* (beginning) and *Kruthi* (performance). This intrinsic nature shapes one's behavior throughout life. The Three Gunas, or cosmic qualities, are:

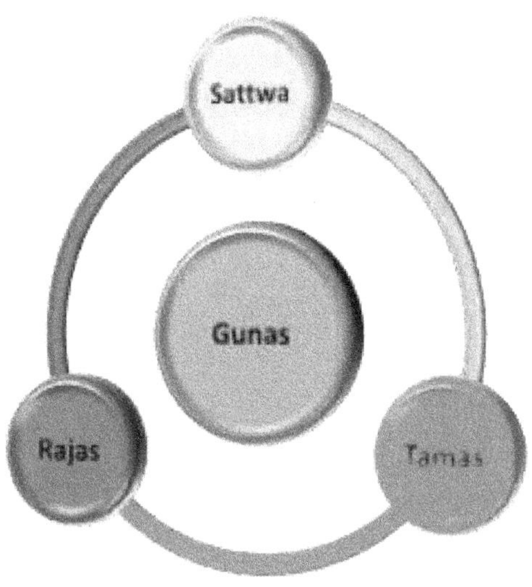

Fig. 8 Types of Gunas

Each Guna has distinct characteristics and influences various aspects of life and behavior.

The Three Gunas

1. Sattwa

- **Characteristics**: Sattwa is the quality of purity, wisdom, and illumination. It promotes happiness, clarity, and a connection with the divine.

- **Behavior and Attributes**: When Sattwa predominates, individuals experience joy and tranquility, and their actions are marked by selflessness and purity. Sattwic individuals seek knowledge, practice self-control, and act with a sense of duty without attachment to results.

- o **Diet and Actions**: Sattwic food is nourishing and pure, such as fresh fruits and vegetables. Acts of charity, sacrifices performed without expectation of reward, and duties done with joy and devotion are Sattwic. The pleasure experienced in Sattwa is akin to nectar, pleasant in its inception and conclusion.

2. Rajas

- o **Characteristics**: Rajas is the quality of passion, activity, and desire. It leads to attachment, restlessness, and the pursuit of pleasure.

- o **Behavior and Attributes**: When Rajas is dominant, individuals are driven by desires and are often restless and greedy. They engage in actions with the expectation of reward and are prone to suffering and discontent. Rajas causes a person to act with intense attachment and to focus on material gains.

- o **Diet and Actions**: Rajasic food is spicy, sour, and stimulating. Sacrifices and actions performed for personal gain, and gifts given with the expectation of return, reflect Rajas. The pleasure derived from Rajas often appears enjoyable at first but turns into suffering in the end.

3. Tamas

- o **Characteristics**: Tamas is the quality of inertia, ignorance, and darkness. It leads to delusion and a lack of clarity.

- o **Behavior and Attributes**: When Tamas prevails, individuals experience lethargy, confusion, and heedlessness. Tamas causes ignorance and a disregard for duty, leading to a lack of motivation and a tendency towards procrastination.

- o **Diet and Actions**: Tamasic food is stale, rotten, and impure. Sacrifices that violate scriptural norms, and gifts given disrespectfully or at inappropriate times, are Tamasic. The pleasure derived from Tamas is deceptive, initially pleasant but ultimately leading to delusion and suffering.

The Four Ashramas

The concept of **Ashramas** represents the four stages of life, each with specific duties and responsibilities that contribute to an individual's evolution and ultimate goal of **Moksha** (liberation). These stages are:

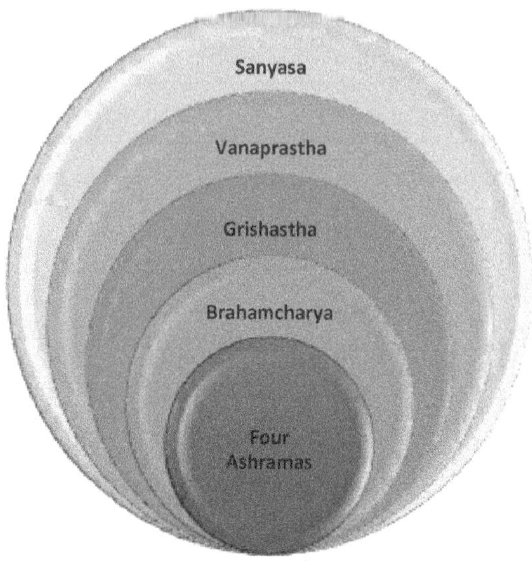

Fig. 9 Types of Ashramas

1. Brahmacharya (Celibacy)

- o **Description**: The first stage, focusing on education and self-discipline. At around age 8, individuals begin their education, which emphasizes character building and knowledge acquisition.

- o **Practices**: Students live a life of celibacy, simplicity, and dedication to their studies. They serve their Guru with respect and avoid indulgence. The Guru imparts wisdom on truth, duty, and dharma.

2. **Grihastha (Householder)** o **Description**: The second stage involves marriage and family life. It is a period of responsibility, including raising a family and fulfilling societal and familial duties.

   o **Practices**: Householders are expected to provide for their family, perform rituals, and practice hospitality. They engage in righteous earning, charity, and uphold moral values while enjoying life's pleasures within ethical limits. They perform five Maha Yajnas (great sacrifices) to maintain harmony and fulfill their duties.

3. **Vanaprastha (Forest-Dweller)**

   o **Description**: This stage marks the transition from active family life to a more contemplative phase. Individuals prepare for renunciation by gradually withdrawing from worldly responsibilities.

   o **Practices**: The focus shifts to living a simple life in nature, reflecting on one's life and duties. Vanaprastha involves detachment from material possessions and responsibilities, preparing for the final stage of Sanyasa.

4. Sannyasa (Renunciation)

- o **Description**: The final stage is characterized by complete renunciation of worldly ties and a focus on spiritual liberation.

- o **Practices**: Sannyasis abandon all material possessions and social ties, living a life of asceticism and devotion. They wander freely, practicing self-discipline and seeking Moksha, transcending all worldly attachments and desires.

Conclusion

The stages of life and the Gunas play pivotal roles in shaping one's journey towards self-realization and spiritual fulfillment. Understanding and applying the principles of the Ashramas and the Gunas can guide individuals through their lives, helping them achieve a balanced and purposeful existence. In today's context, these ancient teachings offer valuable insights into managing life's responsibilities and pursuing spiritual growth.

Chapter 9

Nyaya: The Theory of Knowledge and the Four Pramanas

Introduction

In the realm of Indian philosophy, knowledge is understood as the apprehension of an object, where quality, means, intellect, and apprehension are interconnected facets. The Nyaya theory, often termed **logical realism**, is founded on the belief that knowledge reveals both the knower and the knowable. This theory emphasizes the differentiation between the subject, object, and the means of obtaining valid knowledge.

According to Nyaya philosophy, valid knowledge is termed **Prama**, while invalid knowledge is **Aprama**. The source of valid knowledge is known as **Pramana**. Different Indian philosophical schools accept various methods for acquiring knowledge:

- **Mimamsa** accepts all methods.

- **Yoga** accepts perception, inference, and testimony.

- **Buddhism** and **Vaisesika** accept only perception and inference.

- **Carvaka** accepts only perception.

Nyaya philosophy categorizes cognition into two types: memory and reason. Memory is a state of consciousness resulting from traces of past experiences, while **Anubhava** refers to immediate experiences. Human perception involves both external sense organs (eyes, ears, nose, tongue, skin) and internal faculties (mind), which interact to produce perceptual knowledge.

Sources of Valid Knowledge

Nyaya philosophy identifies four primary sources of valid knowledge:

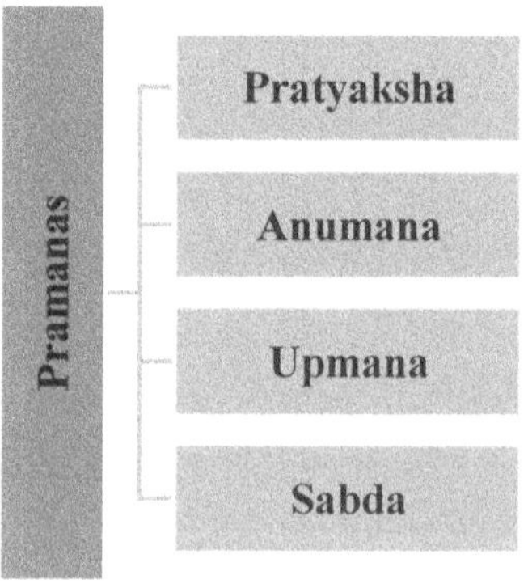

Fig. 10 Four Pramanas

1. Pratyaksha (Perception)

> o **Direct Perception**: This occurs through sensory organs such as sight, hearing, smell, taste, and touch. Direct perception, also known as **Anubhava** or experience, involves direct interaction with external objects.

- o **Indirect Perception**: This is based on memory or past experiences. For example, knowing what grapes look like from past experience helps identify them when seeing similar objects.

2. Anumana (Inference)

- o **Definition**: Inference involves deriving new knowledge from what is already known. It combines two Sanskrit words: *Anu* (after) and *Mana* (knowledge). This process relies on logical reasoning rather than direct sensory experience.

- o **Classification**:

  - **Swarthanumana**: Inference made for personal understanding.

  - **Prarthanumana**: Inference made to convince others.

- o **Example**: Observing smoke on a distant hill leads one to infer the presence of fire, based on the established relationship between smoke and fire.

Inference involves three key terms:

- o **Sadhya**: The character to be inferred (e.g., fire).

- o **Hetu**: The mark used to infer the character (e.g., smoke).

o **Paksha**: The subject where the character is inferred (e.g., the hill).

The invariable relation between Hetu and Sadhya is called **Vyapti**. Knowledge gained through this process is termed **Pramarsa**.

3. Upamana (Analogy or Comparison)

o **Definition**: Upamana involves understanding something new through its similarity to something already known. It is a method of gaining knowledge through analogy.

o **Example**: If someone is unfamiliar with a squirrel but is told it is like a rat with a long tail, seeing such an animal later would allow them to identify it as a squirrel based on this analogy.

4. Sabda (Testimony or Verbal Statement)

o **Definition**: Sabda refers to knowledge obtained through verbal communication from a trustworthy source. The reliability of this source determines the validity of the knowledge.

o **Types**:

- **Vaidika**: Testimony from scriptures or divine sources, considered infallible.

- **Laukika**: Testimony from human sources, which may be fallible but can still be valid if the source is trustworthy.

  o **Example**: A fisherman's advice to a woman about crossing a river is reliable if the fisherman is trustworthy and unbiased.

Conclusion

The Nyaya theory of knowledge provides a structured approach to understanding how knowledge is acquired and validated. Its principles remain relevant in contemporary contexts, offering a framework for evaluating knowledge in everyday life. By applying the methods of Pratyaksha, Anumana, Upamana, and Sabda, one can navigate the complexities of acquiring and validating knowledge effectively.

Chapter 10

Spirituality: An Overview

Introduction

Spirituality encompasses a sense of connection to something greater than ourselves and often involves a quest for meaning in life. It represents a process of personal transformation aligned with traditional religious ideals, engaging in meaningful activities that foster a deep sense of aliveness and interconnectedness. While some associate spirituality with organized religion—such as churches, temples, or mosques—others find solace in a personal relationship with God, nature, or art. Unlike religion, which is specifically connected to God, spirituality pertains to the domain of awareness where values such as truth, love, beauty, and compassion are experienced.

Definitions

"The spiritual dimension tries to be in harmony with the universe, strives for answers about the infinite, and comes into focus when the person faces emotional stress, physical illness, or death."
— Nurses Ruth Beckman Murray and Judith Proctor Zenter

"Spirituality means any experience that is thought to bring the experiencer into contact with the divine (in other words, not just any experience that feels meaningful)."

— Mario Beauregard and Denyse O'Leary

Spirituality is intimately related to the spirit or soul, the life energy within us. Realizing this spirit, often through meditation or religious practice, is the essence of a spiritual life. Spiritual enlightenment involves transcending the mind and ego, which distract from true spirituality. Many seek spiritual awakening and self-realization, but true spiritual enlightenment occurs when we realize we are not merely our bodies or minds, but divine spirits. This realization liberates us from suffering, misery, pain, and the cycle of birth and death.

Spirituality and Ethics in the Bhagavad Gita

Lord Krishna in the Bhagavad Gita highlights the intimate connection between ethics and spirituality, illustrating the relationship between a life of virtue and the attainment of God-realization and liberation. The Bhagavad Gita classifies qualities into two categories:

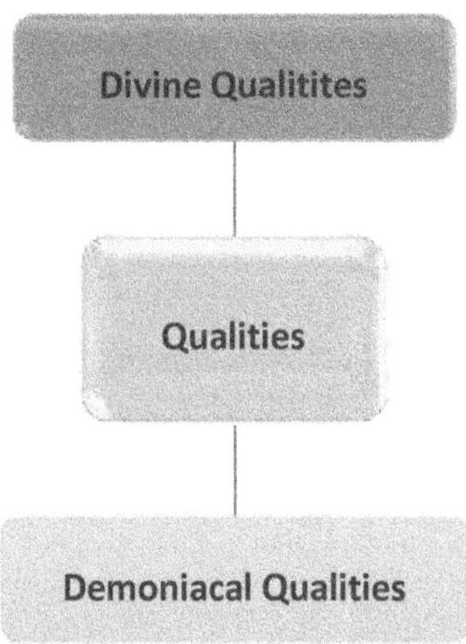

Fig. 11 Types of Qualities

Divine Qualities: These qualities, such as vigor, forgiveness, fortitude, purity, absence of hatred, and absence of pride, are conducive to peace and liberation.

Demoniacal (Undivine) Qualities: These include hypocrisy, arrogance, self-conceit, harshness, and anger, leading to bondage and ignorance of right conduct and truth.

Purity, good conduct, and truth are essential for spiritual progress and an honorable life. According to the Bhagavad Gita, three gates lead to hell: passion, anger, and greed. Liberation and the ultimate goal of life, God-realization, can be achieved by overcoming these traits. **Key Teachings from the Bhagavad Gita**

1. Honor Existence:

The Gita teaches that the universe is composed of eight elements: Earth, Fire, Water, Air, Mind, Intellect, Ether, and Consciousness. Recognizing our interconnectedness with these elements fosters a sense of dignity and equability.

2. Peaceful Fight:

Krishna advises Arjuna to engage in battle with a peaceful mind, free from hatred, and motivated by justice and equability. This teaches us to approach life's challenges with inner peace and righteousness.

3. Witness the Flow of Time:

Life's events are transient, like air passing by. Krishna encourages us to witness and accept the flow of time without becoming attached to moments, whether pleasant or unpleasant.

4. Mind Your Mind:

The mind is central to bondage and liberation. Through disciplined practice (sadhana), we can control our senses and align the mind with higher spiritual goals, transforming it into an ally rather than an adversary.

5. Karma Yoga:

Karma Yoga emphasizes performing duties responsibly without attachment to rewards. Selfless actions, done as offerings to the divine, lead to liberation and positive outcomes, while selfish actions result in negative consequences.

6. You Are Sukha:

True happiness (Sukha) comes from within, not from external, temporary sources. Recognizing this helps us maintain inner joy regardless of external circumstances.

7. Be Stable-Minded:

A stable-minded person controls their senses and turns inward to realize God. Free from expectations, gain, loss, pleasure, pain, and other dualities, such a person acts without attachment and with equanimity.

8. The Divine Wisdom:

Divine wisdom liberates even the most sinful when one acts without egoism or desire for rewards. Faith in God, scriptures, and the Guru's teachings is essential for spiritual advancement, leading to rapid progress on the spiritual path.

9. Stop Hurting:

Krishna's tough love towards Arjuna before battle exemplifies how wise actions, even if initially painful, are ultimately beneficial. When hurt by others, discern whether it is a release of karma or an ignorant act, and respond with understanding or compassion.

Conclusion

Spirituality involves continual self-examination of physical and mental actions to discern the influence of ego and body consciousness versus the soul's wisdom and divine nature. Life is a battle between dualities—life and death, soul and body, spirit and matter, good and bad. Each person must fight their own battle, not for victory, but for the eternal relationship between the soul and God. The universe and everything within it is an expression of God, who is the ultimate cause and essence of all existence.

Chapter 11

The Spiritual Laws of the Universe

Introduction

Spiritual laws impact every aspect of our lives, teaching us about happiness, well-being, peace, non-violence, truth, and success. Those who understand these laws are often more confident, productive, and reflective than those who are unaware, who may find themselves caught in darkness and hurdles with no ray of hope. Spiritual laws have the capacity to lead us out of pessimism and darkness, guiding our spirit and soul toward the Almighty. By connecting our soul to God, we can achieve inner bliss. Knowledge of these spiritual laws is essential for living a happy and smooth life.

Consider a driver who knows the road to his destination—he will reach it easily without many hurdles. In contrast, a person who knows the destination but not the route will naturally face troubles along the way. Spiritual laws are universal and help individuals meet their goals. These laws are as follows:

The Law of Divine Oneness

This law states that everything in the universe is interconnected. Every action we take impacts another, though sometimes the impact is not immediately apparent. Understanding this law encourages empathy, as we recognize the effects of our actions on others.

The Law of Vibration

Every particle in the universe is in constant motion and carries energy. This applies to everything, from planets to chairs. Each entity has a specific energy frequency. High-energy particles harmonize with higher frequencies, while lowerenergy particles align with lower frequencies. Understanding our energy frequency helps us achieve our goals productively.

The Law of Attraction

According to this law, to attract what we desire, we must be positive, proactive, and loving. Like attracts like, so a pessimistic outlook will lead to negative experiences. By being positive and doing positive things, we attract positivity.

The Law of Inspired Action

This law emphasizes that we must actively pursue our desired goals. The law of attraction and the law of inspired action are deeply connected. To achieve our goals, we must take consistent, positive steps, whether big or small.

The Law of Perpetual Transmutation of Energy

This law states that all energy, whether high or low frequency, is constantly changing. Recognizing this helps us to elicit positive changes in ourselves.

The Law of Relativity

This law highlights the objectivity of things when viewed in isolation. No emotion, action, person, or experience can be considered good or bad until compared with something else. Everything in life has multiple perspectives.

The Law of Polarity

Everything in life has its opposite. If we are facing drastic situations, this law reminds us that good developments are also on the way. Understanding this law helps us navigate bad situations more easily.

The Law of Rhythm

All things in the universe come in cycles, whether it's joy and sorrow, seasons, or life cycles. We should appreciate the current phase, as nothing is permanent. Embrace what you have while it lasts.

The Law of Gender

There are two main energies in the universe: feminine and masculine. A balance between these energies is essential for a happy and realistic life, as both play key roles in different aspects.

The Law of Action and Reaction

Every action has an equal and opposite reaction. If we radiate joy, we receive joy in return. Conversely, if we cause pain to others, we will face consequences. This law reminds us to perform good actions to receive positive outcomes.

The Law of Karma

This law emphasizes performing good deeds and maintaining a good nature. Good karma brings favorable results, while bad karma leads to unfavorable circumstances. Serve, love, respect, and make others happy to shape a positive destiny.

The Law of Causation

This law maintains the inner harmony and logical order of the universe. Every cause has an effect, and every effect has a cause. Understanding this helps us see the connection between our actions and their outcomes.

The Law of Compensation

This law operates universally, ensuring balance between cause and effect. Good actions lead to rewards, while bad actions result in consequences. Our life is connected to past and future karmas, influencing our current circumstances.

The Law of Retribution

For every wrong action, there is punishment. Ignorance and negative impulses lead to wicked actions, resulting in regret later. Avoid sowing seeds that yield unpleasant fruits. Perform good deeds, purify thoughts, and attach your soul to God to attain God-consciousness and become a law-giver.

The Law of Resistance

Our mind is a bundle of impressions formed by our senses and actions. Virtuous actions create good impressions, leading to a strong and pure character. By eradicating bad habits and cultivating good ones, we can build a positive character.

Conclusion

These universal or spiritual laws of nature, when followed in daily life, connect our inner soul to God, leading to Godconsciousness. By radiating happiness through good deeds, we free ourselves from the cycle of birth and death and achieve inner bliss. At that point, these laws no longer operate on us.

Chapter 12

Yoga and Meditation: Tools for Stress Management

Introduction

'Yoga' is a Sanskrit word meaning "to join" or unite. The primary purpose of yoga is to unite the body, mind, and spirit in a harmonious way. Yoga is helpful in releasing stress through various postures, breathing techniques, and meditation. It aids in the development of knowledge, spiritual awakening, and spiritual progress. By practicing yoga, one can delve deeper into the physical experience, become more connected with oneself, and be less influenced by anxiety and stress.

Yoga can be performed by anyone of any age, offering various benefits, such as:

Physical Benefits

- Better sleep

- Better balance

- Greater flexibility

- Improved posture

- Stronger immune system

- Increased vitality

- Reduced hypertension

- Decreased cholesterol **Mental Benefits**

- Inner well-being

- Calmness

- Positivity

- Reduced depression and anxiety

- Improved concentration

- Self-acceptance

- Increased social skills

- Greater confidence

The aim of yoga is self-realization, to overcome all kinds of suffering, leading to Moksha (liberation). Shiva is seen as the first Yogi, or Adiyogi, in yogic lore. Several thousand years ago, on the banks of Kantisarovar in the Himalayas, Adiyogi imparted his profound knowledge to seven sages, who carried this powerful yogic science to different parts of the world, including Asia, the Middle East, Northern Africa, and South America. It was in India that the yogic system found its fullest expression.

Though yoga was practiced in the pre-Vedic period, the great sage Maharishi Patanjali systematized and codified existing yoga practices, their meanings, and related knowledge through the Yoga Sutras.

The education of yoga is provided by experienced and knowledgeable individuals. It is said that a person who is clean, good, balanced, truthful, and transparent will be more useful to their family, society, nation, nature, and humanity.

The Fundamentals of Yoga Sadhana

Yoga unites the body, mind, and spirit, giving rise to four broad classifications of Yoga:

Fig. 12 Fundamentals of Yoga Sadhna

- **Karma Yoga**: Utilizes the body.

- **Bhakti Yoga**: Utilizes the emotions.

- **Gyana Yoga**: Utilizes the mind and intellect.

- **Kriya Yoga**: Utilizes energy.

The Yoga of Meditation

Lord Krishna in the Bhagavad Gita stated that only a purified mind, free from desires, can engage in constant meditation on the Atman (soul). The lower self must be controlled by the higher self. One who has perfect control over their body unites with God and sees God in every object and being, finding no difference between gold and stone.

For meditation, one should find a quiet spot free from disturbances, sit comfortably with the head, neck, and spine erect but not tense. Practicing Brahmacharya (celibacy) is necessary for success in meditation. Aspirants are advised to modify their daily habits of eating, sleeping, and recreation, avoiding extremes. This change in life helps accumulate forces and direct the mind to the inner self, transforming the intellect and senses, and merging with the blissful inner self, the Atman. The bliss of the Atman is incomparable.

Meditation

Meditation is an excellent way to reduce stress. It activates a relaxation response by redirecting thoughts away from oneself. According to Dr. John W. Denninger, "Meditation trains the brain to achieve sustained focus and to return to that focus when negative thinking, emotions, and physical sensations intrude—which happens a lot when you feel stressed and anxious." Meditation has been found to change specific areas of the brain linked with depression.

What is Stress?

The life we live today is full of stress, which can stem from various aspects, such as career, occupation, family, financial issues, role ambiguity, pollution, and work overload. We all experience stress daily.

Formally defined, "Stress is an adaptive response, mediated by individual characteristics and/or psychological processes, that is a consequence of any external action, situation, or event that places special physical and/or psychological demands upon a person." According to Walter Cannon, "we need stress to help us with an acute response such as in the 'fight or flight' response."

In stress, we react physically, mentally, and emotionally to various conditions, demands, and changes in our lives. Stress is different for different individuals.

Stressors: Causes that Produce Stress

Stressors are environmental factors that cause stress and can be classified into four types:

- **Individual-Level Stressors**: Directly related to the individual's job or work, such as role conflict and work overload.

- **Group-Level Stressors**: Related to group dynamics and managerial behavior, such as lack of motivation and concern.

- **Organizational Stressors**: Caused by organizational culture or climate, such as organization design, workforce diversity, and improper working environments.

- **Extra-Organizational Stressors**: Caused by factors outside the organization, such as social status, work status, and economic status.

Outcomes of Stress

Stress has behavioral, physiological, and cognitive outcomes, such as absenteeism, turnover, and hypertension. Some symptoms of stress include:

- Depression

- Tiredness

- Anxiety

- Lack of concentration

- Headaches

- Irritation

- Fatigue

- Insomnia

- Anger

- Dissatisfaction

Stress Management through Yoga

There are various techniques in yoga through which stress can be alleviated. These techniques can be used individually or collectively to get relief from extreme stress. Yoga helps in relieving both physical and psychological stress, ensuring a healthy and productive response to stress triggers. Major effects of yoga on the body include:

- Significant effect on the parasympathetic nervous system, assisting in lowering heartbeat and high blood pressure.

- Reduced oxygen demand in the body.

- Improved digestion and strengthened immune system.

- Release of toxic wastes from the body.

- Increased lung capacity.

- Reduced chances of stress, anxiety, and depression.

- Progressive relaxation through body postures, stretching movements, and breathing exercises.

Pranayama, a breathing technique in yoga, is beneficial for reducing stress. Inhaling and exhaling through nostrils and mouth helps relieve stress and high blood pressure, leaving the mind and inner self unburdened.

Stress Management through Meditation

Herbert Benson, a Harvard Medical Doctor, analyzed many meditation programs and derived a four-step relaxation response:

1. Find a quiet environment.

2. Use a mental device, such as a pleasant image or scenery, to shift your mind from unpleasant thoughts.

3. Neglect distracting thoughts by adopting a passive attitude.

4. Sit in a comfortable position.

Practicing this exercise twice a day for ten to twenty minutes before breakfast and dinner can lead to favorable reductions in blood pressure, anxiety, and hypertension, and improve sleep quality. Meditation helps many people control their reactions to stress and its causes, often leading to a reduction in depression and suicidal tendencies.

Conclusion

Yoga and meditation are beneficial techniques for stress management. People worldwide are experiencing the positive effects of these practices, as they help reduce negative thoughts and stressful feelings, leading to a cheerful life.

Chapter 13

The Role of Service and Seva: Giving Back to Society

Introduction

Service, or "seva" as it is referred to in Sanskrit, is a fundamental principle in many spiritual and philosophical traditions. It embodies the act of selfless service to others, driven by compassion and a genuine desire to contribute to the well-being of society. Seva is not merely an act of charity but a profound spiritual practice that nurtures both the giver and the receiver. This chapter delves into the concept of seva, its significance, and its transformative power in individual lives and the broader community.

Understanding Seva

Seva, in its essence, is about giving without expecting anything in return. It transcends the boundaries of race, religion, and socio-economic status, focusing purely on the act of giving from the heart. Seva can take many forms, from simple acts of kindness to organized volunteer work, but the underlying intention remains the same: to serve humanity selflessly.

In many Eastern traditions, particularly in Hinduism, Buddhism, and Sikhism, seva is seen as a path to spiritual growth and enlightenment. It is believed that through serving others, individuals can overcome their ego, develop humility, and foster a sense of unity with all beings. Seva is not just about physical acts but also about offering emotional and spiritual support.

Historical and Cultural Context of Seva

Historically, the concept of seva has been deeply embedded in Indian culture. Ancient texts and scriptures, such as the Bhagavad Gita, emphasize the importance of selfless action. In the Gita, Lord Krishna advises Arjuna to perform his duty without attachment to the results, highlighting the essence of seva.

In Sikhism, seva is a core principle. The Sikh Gurus emphasized the importance of selfless service, and this is reflected in practices such as langar (community kitchen), where volunteers prepare and serve free meals to all visitors regardless of their background. This tradition of seva continues to be a cornerstone of Sikh community life.

The Spiritual Significance of Seva

The practice of seva is not just about benefiting others but also about personal spiritual growth. Engaging in seva helps individuals cultivate virtues such as compassion, empathy, and humility. It encourages a shift from a self-centered perspective to a more expansive view of life, where the welfare of others becomes a priority.

Through seva, individuals can experience a sense of fulfillment and purpose. Serving others provides an opportunity to connect with the deeper aspects of oneself and to experience the joy that comes from giving. This joy is often described as more profound and lasting than the happiness derived from material possessions or achievements.

Seva in Modern Society

In contemporary society, the practice of seva remains relevant and vital. Despite the advancements in technology and the increase in material wealth, many people continue to experience loneliness, stress, and a lack of purpose. Seva offers a pathway to address these issues by fostering a sense of community and interconnectedness.

Volunteering in various capacities, such as working at shelters, participating in environmental clean-ups, or offering professional skills to non-profits, are modern expressions of seva. These acts of service not only help those in need but also enrich the lives of the volunteers, providing them with a sense of accomplishment and connection.

The Impact of Seva on Society

The impact of seva on society is profound. When individuals come together to serve, they create a ripple effect that can lead to significant positive change. Communities that embrace the spirit of seva tend to be more cohesive, resilient, and supportive.

Seva also promotes social equity and justice. By addressing the needs of the marginalized and underserved, acts of service help bridge gaps and reduce inequalities. This fosters a more inclusive society where everyone has the opportunity to thrive.

Personal Stories of Seva

To illustrate the transformative power of seva, let's consider a few personal stories:

1. **The Healing Power of Seva**: A retired doctor, Dr. Asha, found a new sense of purpose in her golden years by offering free medical camps in rural areas. Her efforts not only provided much-needed healthcare to underserved communities but also rekindled her passion for medicine and deepened her sense of empathy and gratitude.

2. **Community Building Through Seva**: In a bustling city, a group of young professionals started a weekend

initiative to clean local parks and plant trees. This not only beautified the environment but also created a strong sense of community among the volunteers, who felt a shared responsibility for their surroundings.

3. **Seva and Personal Transformation**: John, a corporate executive, felt a sense of emptiness despite his professional success. Volunteering at a local homeless shelter transformed his outlook on life. Through seva, he found deeper meaning and satisfaction, leading him to incorporate principles of compassion and service into his daily life and work.

Conclusion

Seva, or selfless service, is a timeless principle that holds immense value in both personal and societal contexts. It is a practice that transcends cultural and religious boundaries, offering a pathway to spiritual growth and a means to create a more compassionate and equitable world. By embracing seva, individuals can find deeper meaning and fulfillment, while collectively contributing to the well-being of society.

In today's fast-paced and often disconnected world, the practice of seva serves as a reminder of our shared humanity and the power of giving. It encourages us to look beyond ourselves and to act with kindness and compassion, fostering a spirit of unity and love. As we engage in acts of service, we not only uplift others but also elevate our own spirits, creating a cycle of positivity and transformation that benefits all.

Chapter 14

Self-Realization and Enlightenment: The Journey Within

Introduction

Self-realization and enlightenment represent the pinnacle of spiritual development in many philosophical and religious traditions. These concepts involve deep understanding and profound inner transformation, leading to the ultimate realization of one's true nature and the nature of reality. This chapter explores the paths to self-realization and enlightenment, the practices that support this journey, and the transformative effects these states of being can have on individuals and society.

Understanding Self-Realization

Self-realization is the recognition of one's true self beyond the ego and the superficial identity shaped by societal influences. It involves an awakening to one's inner divinity, the eternal aspect of the self that is connected to the universal consciousness. In various spiritual traditions, self-realization is considered the ultimate goal of human existence.

Pathways to Self-Realization

1. **Jnana Yoga (Path of Knowledge)**: Jnana Yoga emphasizes the pursuit of wisdom and knowledge as a means to realize the self. Practitioners engage in deep contemplation and study of spiritual texts to

discern the difference between the transient ego and the eternal self. The process involves self-inquiry (Atma Vichara), where one constantly asks, "Who am I?" to peel away layers of false identity.

2. **Bhakti Yoga (Path of Devotion)**: Bhakti Yoga focuses on devotion and love for the divine. Through practices such as chanting, prayer, and rituals, practitioners cultivate a deep emotional connection with a higher power. This devotion helps dissolve the ego and fosters a sense of unity with the divine.

3. **Karma Yoga (Path of Selfless Action)**: Karma Yoga involves performing one's duties and actions without attachment to the outcomes. By dedicating all actions to the divine and practicing selfless service (Seva), individuals purify their hearts and minds, leading to self-realization.

4. **Raja Yoga (Path of Meditation)**: Raja Yoga, also known as the royal path, emphasizes meditation and mental discipline. It involves practices like asanas (postures), pranayama (breath control), and dhyana (meditation) to achieve a state of inner stillness and self-awareness. The ultimate goal is to transcend the mind and experience the true self.

Understanding Enlightenment

Enlightenment, often used interchangeably with self-realization, represents the culmination of spiritual awakening. It is the state of being where one transcends individual consciousness and merges with the universal consciousness. Enlightenment is characterized by profound wisdom, compassion, and a sense of oneness with all existence.

Practices Leading to Enlightenment

1. **Meditation**: Meditation is a fundamental practice on the path to enlightenment. It involves focusing the mind and turning inward to experience the stillness and silence within. Through regular meditation, individuals can transcend the ego and experience the unity of all life.

2. **Mindfulness**: Mindfulness is the practice of being fully present in the moment. It involves observing thoughts, emotions, and sensations without judgment. By cultivating mindfulness, individuals can develop greater self-awareness and connect with their true nature.

3. **Compassion and Loving-Kindness**: Compassion and loving-kindness practices help expand one's sense of self to include others. By developing a heart full of love and compassion, individuals can transcend the ego and experience a deep connection with all beings.

4. **Self-Inquiry**: Self-inquiry, as taught by sages like Ramana Maharshi, involves questioning the nature of the self. By continuously asking "Who am I?" and examining the source of one's thoughts and identity, practitioners can dissolve the ego and realize their true nature.

Transformative Effects of Self-Realization and Enlightenment

1. **Inner Peace and Contentment**: Self-realization and enlightenment bring a profound sense of inner peace and contentment. Individuals no longer seek fulfillment from external sources but find it within

themselves. This inner peace remains unshaken by external circumstances.

2. **Compassion and Empathy**: Enlightened beings possess boundless compassion and empathy. They see themselves in others and are naturally inclined to help alleviate the suffering of all beings. This profound sense of connection fosters a more compassionate and harmonious society.

3. **Wisdom and Clarity**: Enlightenment brings unparalleled wisdom and clarity. Individuals gain deep insights into the nature of reality, understanding the interconnectedness of all life. This wisdom guides their actions, leading to more ethical and purposeful living.

4. **Fearlessness and Freedom**: The realization of one's true nature dissolves fear and insecurity. Enlightened individuals live with a sense of freedom, unbound by the limitations of the ego. They embrace life with openness and courage.

Real-Life Examples of Enlightened Beings

1. **Gautama Buddha**: Siddhartha Gautama, known as the Buddha, attained enlightenment through deep meditation and self-inquiry. His teachings on the Four Noble Truths and the Eightfold Path provide a practical guide for achieving enlightenment and liberation from suffering.

2. **Ramana Maharshi**: An Indian sage, Ramana Maharshi advocated the practice of self-inquiry to realize the true self. His teachings emphasize the

importance of asking "Who am I?" and turning inward to experience the self's true nature.

3. **Mahatma Gandhi**: Although not typically described as an enlightened being in the traditional sense, Mahatma Gandhi's life exemplified the principles of self-realization and enlightenment. His commitment to truth, nonviolence, and selfless service transformed the lives of millions and demonstrated the power of living in alignment with one's higher self.

Integrating Self-Realization and Enlightenment into Daily Life

1. **Daily Meditation Practice**: Establishing a regular meditation practice helps cultivate inner stillness and self-awareness. Even a few minutes of daily meditation can have a profound impact on one's journey toward self-realization.

2. **Mindful Living**: Practicing mindfulness in everyday activities, such as eating, walking, and working, helps maintain a connection with the present moment. This awareness fosters a deeper understanding of oneself and the world.

3. **Selfless Service**: Engaging in acts of selfless service (Seva) helps dissolve the ego and cultivate a sense of unity with others. Volunteering, helping those in need, and contributing to the community are practical ways to practice selflessness.

4. **Study of Spiritual Texts**: Reading and contemplating spiritual texts from various traditions can provide valuable insights and inspiration on the path to self-realization and enlightenment. Texts such

as the Bhagavad Gita, the Tao Te Ching, and the works of mystics like Rumi offer profound wisdom.

Conclusion

The journey to self-realization and enlightenment is a deeply personal and transformative process. By exploring various pathways and practices, individuals can awaken to their true nature and experience a profound sense of inner peace, wisdom, and compassion. While the journey may be challenging, the rewards of self-realization and enlightenment are boundless, offering not only personal fulfillment but also contributing to a more harmonious and compassionate world. As we embark on this journey within, we discover that the true essence of our being is interconnected with all of existence, leading us to a life of purpose, love, and profound inner peace.

Chapter 15

Mindfulness and Compassion: Cultivating Inner Peace

Introduction

In the fast-paced and often stressful world we live in, finding inner peace can be challenging. However, mindfulness and compassion offer powerful tools to help us navigate life's difficulties and cultivate a sense of tranquility and well-being. This chapter explores the concepts of mindfulness and compassion, their benefits, and practical ways to integrate these practices into daily life to achieve inner peace.

Understanding Mindfulness

Mindfulness is the practice of paying deliberate attention to the present moment without judgment. It involves being fully aware of our thoughts, emotions, bodily sensations, and surroundings. Mindfulness has its roots in Buddhist meditation practices but has gained widespread recognition and application in secular contexts due to its numerous mental and physical health benefits.

The Benefits of Mindfulness

<table>
<tr><td>Stress Reduction</td><td>Improved Emotional Intelligence</td></tr>
<tr><td>Enhanced Focus and Concentration</td><td>Better Physical Health</td></tr>
</table>

1. **Stress Reduction**: One of the most significant benefits of mindfulness is its ability to reduce stress. By focusing on the present moment, individuals can break the cycle of worrying about the future or ruminating on the past, which are common sources of stress.

2. **Improved Emotional Regulation**: Mindfulness helps individuals become more aware of their emotions and reactions, allowing them to respond to situations more calmly and thoughtfully rather than reacting impulsively.

3. **Enhanced Focus and Concentration**: Regular mindfulness practice can improve attention and concentration, making it easier to stay focused on tasks and improve productivity.

4. **Better Physical Health**: Mindfulness has been shown to lower blood pressure, improve sleep

quality, and boost the immune system, contributing to overall better physical health.

Understanding Compassion

Compassion involves recognizing the suffering of others and having a desire to alleviate it. It goes beyond empathy, which is the ability to understand and share the feelings of another, by including a motivation to take action to help. Selfcompassion, on the other hand, involves treating oneself with the same kindness and understanding that one would offer to a friend in distress.

The Benefits of Compassion

1. **Emotional Resilience**: Compassionate individuals tend to be more resilient in the face of adversity. By fostering positive emotions and a supportive mindset, compassion helps build emotional strength.

2. **Enhanced Relationships**: Practicing compassion strengthens interpersonal relationships by fostering understanding, empathy, and cooperation. It encourages a supportive and nurturing environment.

3. **Greater Happiness**: Compassionate actions and thoughts can increase levels of happiness and life satisfaction. Acts of kindness and altruism trigger the release of endorphins, the brain's natural feel-good chemicals.

4. **Reduced Negative Emotions**: Compassion helps reduce negative emotions such as anger, resentment, and jealousy. By focusing on the well-being of others, individuals can shift their perspective and cultivate a more positive outlook.

Integrating Mindfulness and Compassion into Daily Life

Combining mindfulness and compassion practices can create a powerful synergy that enhances inner peace and overall wellbeing. Here are some practical ways to incorporate these practices into daily life:

1. **Mindful Breathing**: A simple yet effective mindfulness practice involves focusing on your breath. Set aside a few minutes each day to sit quietly and pay attention to your inhalations and exhalations. Notice the sensations of the breath entering and leaving your body. When your mind wanders, gently bring your focus back to your breath.

2. **Body Scan Meditation**: This practice involves lying down or sitting comfortably and bringing attention to different parts of your body, starting from your toes and moving up to your head. Notice any sensations, tensions, or areas of relaxation. The body scan helps increase body awareness and promotes relaxation.

3. **Loving-Kindness Meditation**: This compassionbased meditation involves silently repeating phrases such as "May I be happy, may I be healthy, may I be safe, may I live with ease." After offering these wishes to yourself, extend them to others, including loved ones, acquaintances, and even those with whom you have difficulties.

4. **Gratitude Journaling**: Cultivating a sense of gratitude can enhance mindfulness and compassion. Each day, write down three things you are grateful for. Reflecting on positive aspects of your life helps shift your focus away from stress and negativity.

5. **Compassionate Listening**: Practice active and empathetic listening in your interactions with others. Pay full attention to the speaker, acknowledge their feelings, and respond with kindness and understanding. Compassionate listening strengthens relationships and fosters a supportive environment.

6. **Mindful Walking**: Turn a regular walk into a mindfulness practice by paying attention to the sensations of walking. Notice the feeling of your feet touching the ground, the movement of your legs, and the rhythm of your breath. Walking mindfully can be a grounding and calming experience.

7. **Self-Compassion Practices**: Treat yourself with kindness, especially during challenging times. When you make a mistake or face a setback, remind yourself that it is part of being human. Practice selfcompassion by offering yourself words of encouragement and understanding.

Scientific Evidence Supporting Mindfulness and Compassion

Research has extensively documented the benefits of mindfulness and compassion practices. Studies have shown that mindfulness meditation can lead to structural changes in the brain, including increased gray matter density in regions associated with learning, memory, and emotional regulation. These changes contribute to improved cognitive function and emotional well-being.

Similarly, research on compassion has demonstrated its positive impact on mental health. Compassionate individuals tend to experience lower levels of anxiety and depression, and higher levels of life satisfaction. The practice of selfcompassion has been linked to greater emotional resilience and reduced stress.

Challenges and Misconceptions

While mindfulness and compassion practices offer numerous benefits, there can be challenges and misconceptions:

1. **Misconception of Mindfulness as Escapism**: Some people may view mindfulness as a way to escape from reality or avoid problems. In reality, mindfulness involves facing and accepting the present moment with clarity and openness.

2. **Challenges of Consistency**: Integrating mindfulness and compassion practices into daily life requires consistency and dedication. It can be challenging to maintain regular practice, especially during busy or stressful times.

3. **Self-Judgment in Mindfulness Practice**: Beginners may struggle with self-judgment when their minds wander during mindfulness practice. It's important to remember that mind-wandering is natural, and gently bringing attention back to the present moment is part of the practice.

Conclusion

Mindfulness and compassion are powerful tools for cultivating inner peace and well-being. By being present in the moment and treating ourselves and others with kindness and understanding, we can navigate life's challenges with greater ease and resilience. Integrating these practices into daily life requires commitment, but the benefits are profound, leading to improved mental and physical health, enhanced relationships, and a deeper sense of fulfillment. As we embrace mindfulness and compassion, we create a ripple effect that not only transforms our own lives but also positively impacts those around us.

94

Chapter 16

Ethical Leadership: Leading with Integrity and Wisdom

Introduction

Ethical leadership is the practice of leading an organization or community in a manner that respects ethical principles and values. It involves guiding others with integrity, honesty, fairness, and wisdom. In today's complex and rapidly changing world, ethical leadership is more crucial than ever. This chapter explores the principles of ethical leadership, the qualities that define ethical leaders, and the impact of ethical leadership on organizations and society.

Principles of Ethical Leadership

Ethical leadership is founded on several key principles that guide the behavior and decisions of leaders:

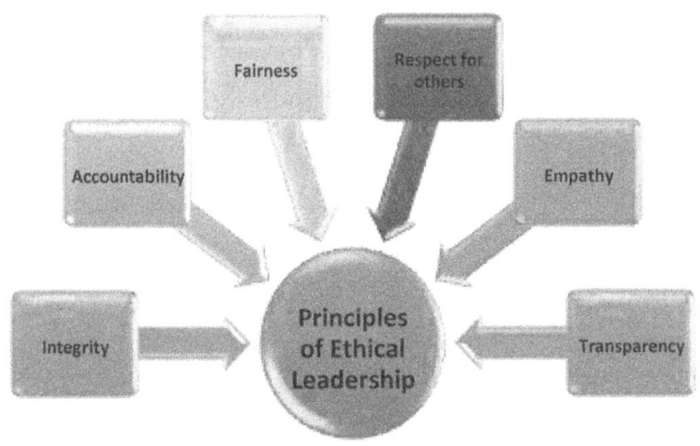

Fig. 13 Principles of Ethicsal Leadership

1. **Integrity**: Integrity involves being honest and having strong moral principles. An ethical leader consistently demonstrates integrity by being truthful and transparent in their actions and decisions.

2. **Accountability**: Ethical leaders hold themselves and others accountable for their actions. They take responsibility for their decisions and the outcomes of those decisions, ensuring that they align with ethical standards.

3. **Fairness**: Fairness is a core principle of ethical leadership. Leaders must treat all individuals with respect and without favoritism or discrimination. This includes making decisions that are just and equitable.

4. **Respect for Others**: Ethical leaders value and respect the dignity and rights of all individuals. They listen to diverse perspectives, foster inclusive environments, and encourage collaboration.

5. **Empathy**: Empathy allows leaders to understand and share the feelings of others. Ethical leaders demonstrate empathy by considering the impact of their decisions on various stakeholders and showing compassion in their interactions.

6. **Transparency**: Transparency involves openly sharing information and being clear about the decision-making processes. Ethical leaders practice transparency to build trust and credibility.

Qualities of Ethical Leaders

Several qualities distinguish ethical leaders from others:

1. **Courage**: Ethical leaders possess the courage to make difficult decisions, even when those decisions may be unpopular or face resistance. They stand up for what

   is right, even in the face of adversity.

2. **Humility**: Humility is a hallmark of ethical leadership. Humble leaders recognize their limitations, seek input from others, and acknowledge their mistakes. They prioritize the collective good over personal ego.

3. **Vision**: Ethical leaders have a clear and inspiring vision for the future. They communicate this vision effectively and align their actions with their values and goals.

4. **Decisiveness**: Ethical leaders are decisive, making well-considered decisions promptly. They balance careful analysis with timely action, ensuring that ethical considerations are integrated into their decision-making process.

5. **Commitment to Ethical Standards**: Ethical leaders are unwavering in their commitment to ethical standards. They consistently uphold these standards, setting a positive example for others to follow.

Impact of Ethical Leadership on Organizations

Ethical leadership has a profound impact on organizations, influencing various aspects such as culture, performance, and reputation:

1. **Organizational Culture**: Ethical leadership fosters a positive organizational culture characterized by trust, respect, and collaboration. When leaders model ethical behavior, it sets a standard for the entire organization, encouraging employees to act with integrity and accountability.

2. **Employee Engagement and Retention**: Employees are more likely to be engaged and committed to an organization that is led by ethical leaders. They feel valued andrespected, which leads to higher job satisfaction and lower turnover rates.

3. **Reputation and Trust**: Ethical leadership enhances an organization's reputation and builds trust with stakeholders, including customers, investors, and the community. Trust is a critical asset that can lead to long-term success and resilience.

4. **Decision-Making and Innovation**: Ethical leaders create an environment where ethical considerations are integral to the decision-making process. This approach encourages innovation, as employees feel safe to propose new ideas and solutions without fear of ethical compromises.

Ethical Leadership in Practice

To illustrate the practical application of ethical leadership, let's examine a few real-world examples:

1. **Case Study: Patagonia**: Patagonia, an outdoor apparel company, is renowned for its ethical leadership. Founder Yvon Chouinard has emphasized environmental sustainability and social responsibility, integrating these values into the company's

operations. Patagonia's commitment to ethical practices has not only enhanced its brand reputation but also inspired other companies to adopt similar values.

2. **Case Study: Johnson & Johnson**: Johnson & Johnson's handling of the Tylenol crisis in 1982 is a classic example of ethical leadership. When cyanidelaced Tylenol capsules led to several deaths, the company's leadership prioritized customer safety over profits. They recalled millions of bottles of Tylenol and introduced tamper-evident packaging, setting new industry standards and restoring public trust.

3. **Case Study: Starbucks**: Starbucks' commitment to ethical sourcing and fair trade practices reflects its ethical leadership. By ensuring that coffee farmers are paid fair wages and supporting sustainable farming practices, Starbucks demonstrates its dedication to social and environmental responsibility.

Developing Ethical Leadership

Developing ethical leadership requires intentional effort and continuous learning. Here are some strategies for cultivating ethical leadership:

1. **Education and Training**: Provide leaders with education and training on ethical principles and decision-making. This includes workshops, seminars, and courses on ethics, corporate social responsibility, and leadership development.

2. **Mentorship and Role Models**: Encourage leaders to seek mentorship from experienced ethical leaders.

Role models can provide guidance, share insights, and inspire ethical behavior.

3. **Ethical Frameworks and Policies**: Establish clear ethical frameworks and policies within the organization. These should outline expected behaviors, decision-making processes, and mechanisms for addressing ethical dilemmas.

4. **Self-Reflection and Accountability**: Encourage leaders to engage in self-reflection and seek feedback on their actions. Accountability mechanisms, such as ethical audits and performance reviews, can help ensure that leaders adhere to ethical standards.

5. **Fostering a Culture of Ethics**: Create a culture that prioritizes ethics by recognizing and rewarding ethical behavior. Encourage open dialogue about ethical issues and provide channels for reporting unethical conduct.

Conclusion

Ethical leadership is essential for creating organizations and societies that thrive on integrity, trust, and respect. By embodying the principles of ethical leadership and cultivating the qualities of courage, humility, and vision, leaders can inspire positive change and contribute to the greater good. The impact of ethical leadership extends beyond the immediate organization, influencing the broader community and setting a standard for future generations. As we navigate the complexities of the modern world, ethical leadership serves as a guiding light, reminding us of the power of leading with integrity and wisdom.

Chapter 17

The Power of Intention: Manifesting a Purposeful Life

Introduction

Intention is a powerful force that shapes our lives in profound ways. It is the driving energy behind our actions, guiding us toward our goals and dreams. When we set clear, purposeful intentions, we align our thoughts, emotions, and actions, creating a pathway to manifest our desired reality. This chapter explores the essence of intention, its impact on our lives, and practical ways to harness its power for a purposeful life.

Understanding Intention

Intention is more than a simple wish or desire; it is a focused and directed energy that sets the stage for our actions and outcomes. Unlike fleeting thoughts or passing wishes, a true intention is imbued with clarity, commitment, and emotional investment. It is a declaration to ourselves and the universe about what we aim to achieve.

Intention is closely linked to our values and beliefs. When our intentions align with our core values, they become a powerful motivator, driving us to act in ways that are congruent with our authentic selves. This alignment creates a sense of purpose and fulfillment, as we feel that our actions are meaningful and significant.

The Science of Intention

Scientific research has begun to uncover the mechanisms through which intention influences our lives. Studies in the field of psychology have shown that setting specific, challenging goals can significantly enhance performance and motivation. This phenomenon, known as the goal-setting theory, highlights the importance of having clear intentions.

Moreover, the concept of neuroplasticity—the brain's ability to reorganize itself by forming new neural connections—supports the idea that our thoughts and intentions can shape our reality. When we focus our attention and energy on a specific intention, we activate neural pathways that reinforce this focus, making it easier to achieve our goals.

The Law of Attraction

The law of attraction is a popular concept that underscores the power of intention. According to this principle, like attracts like, meaning that the energy we emit through our thoughts and emotions attracts similar energy into our lives. By setting positive, purposeful intentions, we can attract positive outcomes and experiences.

To harness the law of attraction, it is crucial to cultivate a positive mindset and focus on what we want rather than what we lack. Visualization techniques, where we imagine ourselves achieving our goals and experiencing the associated emotions, can amplify the power of our intentions. This practice helps to embed our intentions into our subconscious mind, aligning our inner world with our desired reality.

Practical   Steps   to   Manifest   Intentions

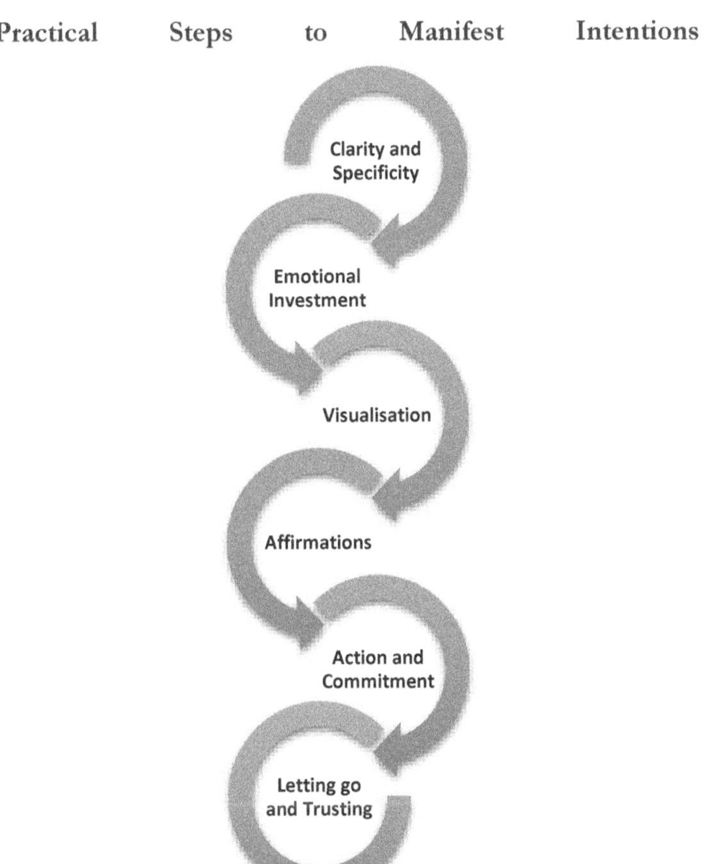

Fig. 14 Practical Steps to Manifest Intentions

1. **Clarity and Specificity**: The first step in manifesting intentions is to gain clarity about what we truly want. Vague or ambiguous intentions are less likely to produce tangible results. Instead, we should define our intentions with specificity, detailing the desired outcome and the steps needed to achieve it.

2. **Emotional Investment**: Intentions are most powerful when they are emotionally charged. We need to connect with our intentions on a deep, emotional level, feeling the excitement, joy, and fulfillment that achieving them will bring. This emotional investment fuels our motivation and perseverance.

3. **Visualization**: Visualization is a potent tool for manifesting intentions. By creating vivid mental images of our desired outcomes, we engage our subconscious mind and reinforce our intentions. Visualization should be practiced regularly, ideally in a relaxed state, to enhance its effectiveness.

4. **Affirmations**: Positive affirmations are statements that reinforce our intentions and beliefs. By repeating affirmations that align with our goals, we can reprogram our subconscious mind and overcome limiting beliefs. For example, if our intention is to cultivate self-confidence, we might repeat affirmations such as "I am confident and capable" or "I believe in my abilities."

5. **Action and Commitment**: While intention is powerful, it must be coupled with action. Setting intentions without taking concrete steps to achieve them is unlikely to yield results. We must commit to our intentions and take consistent, purposeful actions that move us toward our goals. This commitment demonstrates our dedication and signals to the universe that we are serious about manifesting our intentions.

6. **Letting Go and Trusting**: Paradoxically, an essential part of manifesting intentions is learning to let go and trust the process. This does not mean abandoning our goals but rather releasing the need for control and trusting that the universe will support our efforts. Letting

go reduces anxiety and allows us to remain open to opportunities and synchronicities that align with our intentions.

Overcoming Obstacles

Manifesting intentions is not always a smooth journey; obstacles and challenges are inevitable. However, these challenges can be valuable learning experiences that strengthen our resolve and resilience.

1. **Overcoming Limiting Beliefs**: Limiting beliefs are negative thoughts and perceptions that hinder our progress. To overcome these, we must first identify and acknowledge them. Once recognized, we can challenge and reframe these beliefs, replacing them with empowering ones.

2. **Managing Fear and Doubt**: Fear and doubt are natural responses to stepping out of our comfort zones. Rather than avoiding these emotions, we should confront and address them. Techniques such as mindfulness, meditation, and self-compassion can help us manage fear and doubt, allowing us to stay focused on our intentions.

3. **Staying Persistent**: Persistence is crucial in the manifestation process. There will be times when progress seems slow or obstacles appear insurmountable. During these moments, it is essential to stay committed to our intentions and continue taking consistent actions. Persistence, coupled with patience, ensures that we remain on the path to achieving our goals.

Real-Life Examples

Many successful individuals attribute their achievements to the power of intention. Consider the story of Oprah Winfrey, who has often spoken about the role of intention in her life. Despite facing numerous challenges and setbacks, she remained focused on her intentions of personal growth and making a positive impact. Her unwavering commitment to these intentions has led to her remarkable success and influence.

Similarly, the renowned author J.K. Rowling set clear intentions for her writing career, despite facing rejections and financial difficulties. Her perseverance and belief in her intentions eventually resulted in the creation of the immensely popular Harry Potter series, transforming her life and inspiring millions.

Conclusion

The power of intention is a transformative force that can guide us toward a purposeful and fulfilling life. By setting clear, emotionally charged intentions and coupling them with consistent action, we can manifest our desired reality. The journey may present challenges, but with persistence, positivity, and trust, we can overcome obstacles and achieve our goals. Embracing the power of intention allows us to live with purpose, align with our true selves, and create a life that resonates with our deepest values and aspirations.

Chapter 18

Interconnectedness and Harmony: Embracing Unity in Diversity

Introduction

The world is a rich tapestry of diverse cultures, beliefs, and perspectives. Amidst this diversity lies a fundamental truth: we are all interconnected. Embracing this interconnectedness fosters harmony and unity, allowing us to appreciate the richness of our differences while recognizing our shared humanity. This chapter explores the concept of interconnectedness, the benefits of embracing diversity, and practical ways to cultivate unity and harmony in our lives and communities.

The Concept of Interconnectedness

Interconnectedness refers to the intrinsic links that bind individuals, communities, and the natural world. It is the understanding that our actions, thoughts, and emotions have far-reaching impacts, influencing not only ourselves but also others and the environment. This concept is rooted in various philosophical, spiritual, and scientific traditions.

In many spiritual traditions, interconnectedness is a core principle. For example, Buddhism teaches the concept of "dependent origination," which posits that all phenomena arise in dependence upon multiple causes and conditions. Similarly, Indigenous cultures around the world emphasize the sacred relationship between humans, nature, and the cosmos.

Scientifically, interconnectedness is evident in ecosystems, where the balance and health of one species affect the entire system. In human societies, globalization has highlighted how interconnected our economies, cultures, and technologies have become. These interconnections underscore the importance of cooperation, empathy, and mutual respect.

The Value of Diversity

Diversity encompasses the myriad differences that make each individual and community unique, including race, ethnicity, gender, age, religion, abilities, and socioeconomic status. Embracing diversity enriches our lives, broadens our perspectives, and fosters innovation and creativity.

1. **Cultural Enrichment**: Exposure to diverse cultures allows us to experience different traditions, languages, and worldviews. This cultural enrichment deepens our understanding and appreciation of the world's complexity and beauty.

2. **Enhanced Problem-Solving**: Diverse teams bring varied perspectives and experiences to the table, leading to more innovative and effective solutions. Different viewpoints challenge our assumptions and encourage us to think more critically and creatively.

3. **Personal Growth**: Interacting with people from diverse backgrounds fosters empathy, tolerance, and open-mindedness. It challenges us to confront our biases and expand our horizons, promoting personal growth and self-awareness.

4. **Social Cohesion**: Embracing diversity strengthens social cohesion by building bridges between different communities. It fosters a sense of belonging and mutual respect, reducing prejudice and discrimination.

Practical Steps to Embrace Unity in Diversity

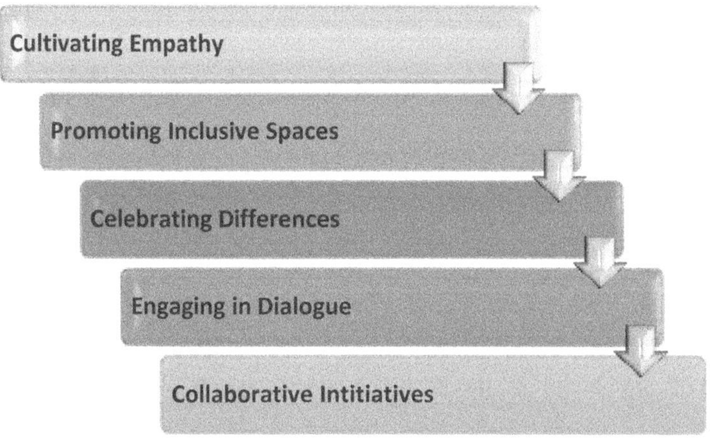

Fig. 15 Practial Steps to Emrace Unity in Diversity

1. **Cultivating Empathy**: Empathy is the ability to understand and share the feelings of others. To cultivate empathy, we must actively listen to others' stories and experiences, seeking to understand their perspectives without judgment. Practicing empathy helps us connect with people on a deeper level, fostering compassion and solidarity.

2. **Promoting Inclusive Spaces**: Creating inclusive environments where everyone feels valued and respected is crucial. This involves recognizing and addressing systemic inequalities, ensuring that diverse voices are heard, and promoting equitable opportunities for all. Inclusive spaces encourage meaningful interactions and collaborations.

3. **Celebrating Differences**: Rather than merely tolerating differences, we should celebrate them. This can be done through cultural events, festivals, and educational

programs that highlight the richness of diverse traditions and practices. Celebrating differences fosters a sense of pride and belonging within diverse communities.

4. **Engaging in Dialogue**: Open and respectful dialogue is essential for bridging divides and building understanding. Engaging in conversations about diversity and inclusion helps us learn from each other and address misconceptions. Dialogue should be approached with curiosity, humility, and a willingness to learn.

5. **Collaborative Initiatives**: Participating in collaborative initiatives that bring together people from diverse backgrounds can strengthen bonds and promote unity. This could include community service projects, intercultural exchange programs, and joint efforts to address social issues. Collaborative initiatives highlight our shared goals and values.

Overcoming Challenges

Embracing unity in diversity is not without its challenges. Prejudice, discrimination, and cultural misunderstandings can create barriers to inclusion and harmony. However, these challenges can be addressed through conscious effort and commitment.

1. **Addressing Prejudice**: Prejudice is often rooted in ignorance and fear. To combat prejudice, we must educate ourselves and others about different cultures, histories, and experiences. This education can dispel myths and stereotypes, fostering a more accurate and nuanced understanding of diversity.

2. **Promoting Equity**: Achieving true unity requires addressing systemic inequalities that disproportionately

affect marginalized communities. This involves advocating for policies and practices that promote equity and justice, ensuring that everyone has access to the same opportunities and resources.

3. **Building Trust**: Trust is the foundation of harmonious relationships. Building trust requires consistent actions that demonstrate respect, honesty, and integrity. It involves being accountable for our actions and showing a genuine commitment to inclusivity.

4. **Embracing Change**: Embracing diversity often requires us to step out of our comfort zones and adapt to new ways of thinking and interacting. This can be challenging, but it is essential for growth and progress. Embracing change with an open mind and heart allows us to evolve and thrive in an interconnected world.

Real-Life Examples

Many organizations and individuals have successfully embraced unity in diversity, demonstrating the transformative power of this approach.

1. **Global Organizations**: Companies like Google and Microsoft have implemented diversity and inclusion initiatives that prioritize equitable hiring practices, employee resource groups, and inclusive workplace cultures. These efforts have not only enhanced innovation and productivity but also created more supportive and collaborative environments.

2. **Community Programs**: Community-based programs such as cultural exchange initiatives and interfaith dialogues have brought together people from different backgrounds to share experiences and build mutual understanding. These programs have fostered a sense of

community and solidarity, reducing tensions and promoting peace.

3. **Educational Institutions**: Schools and universities that prioritize diversity and inclusion create enriching learning environments where students from various backgrounds can thrive. By integrating diverse perspectives into the curriculum and promoting intercultural competence, these institutions prepare students to navigate and contribute to an interconnected world.

Conclusion

Interconnectedness and harmony are essential for creating a world where diversity is embraced and unity is celebrated. By recognizing our interconnectedness, valuing diversity, and actively promoting inclusivity, we can foster a more compassionate, innovative, and cohesive society. Embracing unity in diversity allows us to appreciate the richness of our differences while recognizing our shared humanity, paving the way for a more harmonious and prosperous future.

Chapter 19

Ethical Living: Balancing Personal and Collective Well-being

Introduction

Ethical living involves making choices that reflect our values and principles, balancing our personal well-being with the greater good of society. It requires a deep understanding of the impact of our actions on ourselves and others, as well as a commitment to integrity, compassion, and justice. This chapter explores the principles of ethical living, its benefits, and practical ways to incorporate ethics into our daily lives.

The Principles of Ethical Living

Ethical living is grounded in several core principles that guide our behavior and decision-making. These principles serve as a moral compass, helping us navigate complex situations with a sense of purpose and responsibility.

1. **Integrity**: Integrity involves being honest and consistent in our actions, even when it is difficult. It means staying true to our values and principles, and acting in a way that aligns with them.

2. **Compassion**: Compassion is the ability to empathize with others and act with kindness and understanding. It involves recognizing the suffering of others and taking steps to alleviate it.

3. **Justice**: Justice is the principle of fairness and equity It requires us to advocate for the rights of others, address inequalities, and ensure that everyone is treated with dignity and respect.

4. **Responsibility**: Responsibility involves being accountable for our actions and their consequences. It means considering the impact of our choices on others and the environment, and making decisions that promote the well-being of all.

The Benefits of Ethical Living

Living ethically offers numerous benefits, both for individuals and society as a whole. It fosters a sense of purpose, strengthens relationships, and contributes to a more just and compassionate world.

1. **Personal Fulfillment**: Ethical living aligns our actions with our values, leading to a sense of fulfillment and satisfaction. When we act in accordance with our principles, we experience inner peace and a sense of integrity.

2. **Stronger Relationships**: Ethical behavior builds trust and respect in our relationships. When we act with honesty, compassion, and fairness, we create stronger, more meaningful connections with others.

3. **Social Harmony**: Ethical living promotes social harmony by fostering mutual respect and understanding. It encourages us to consider the needs and rights of others, reducing conflict and promoting cooperation.

4. **Positive Impact**: Ethical choices contribute to the greater good by addressing social and environmental issues. By acting responsibly and advocating for justice,

we can create positive change and improve the well-being of our communities.

Practical Steps to Ethical Living

Incorporating ethical principles into our daily lives requires conscious effort and reflection. The following steps provide a practical framework for ethical living.

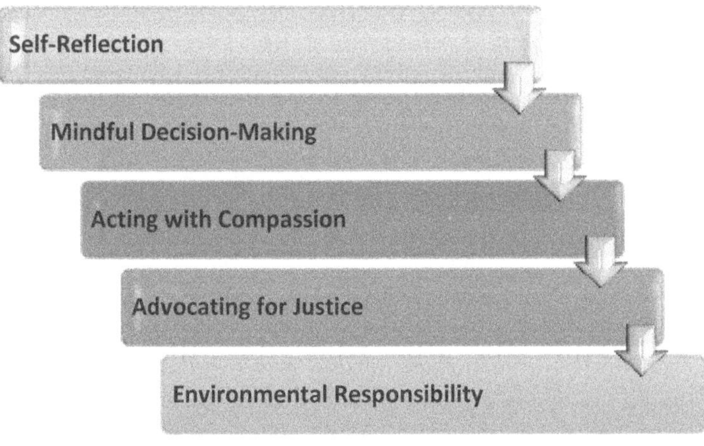

Fig. 16 Practical framework for ethical living.

1. **Self-Reflection**: Ethical living begins with self-reflection. We must regularly examine our values, beliefs, and actions to ensure they align with our principles. This involves being honest with ourselves about our motivations and the impact of our choices.

2. **Mindful Decision-Making**: Ethical living requires mindful decision-making. We must consider the potential consequences of our actions on ourselves and others, and choose the path that aligns with our values and promotes the greater good.

3. **Acting with Compassion**: Compassion is a cornerstone of ethical living. We must strive to act with kindness and empathy, recognizing the humanity in others and taking steps to alleviate suffering.

4. **Advocating for Justice**: Ethical living involves advocating for justice and fairness. We must stand up against injustice, support the rights of others, and work towards a more equitable society.

5. **Environmental Responsibility**: Ethical living extends to our relationship with the environment. We must consider the ecological impact of our choices and strive to live sustainably, reducing our footprint and protecting the natural world.

Overcoming Challenges

Living ethically can be challenging, particularly in a world where unethical behavior is often normalized or rewarded. However, these challenges can be overcome with dedication and resilience.

1. **Addressing Moral Dilemmas**: Moral dilemmas arise when our values conflict or when the right course of action is unclear. To navigate these dilemmas, we must seek guidance from our principles, consult with trusted individuals, and consider the potential consequences of our choices.

2. **Resisting Peer Pressure**: Peer pressure can lead us to compromise our values. To resist this pressure, we must have a strong sense of self and remain committed to our principles, even when it is difficult.

3. **Confronting Injustice**: Standing up against injustice can be daunting, especially when it involves challenging powerful individuals or systems. However, we must find

the courage to speak out and take action, knowing that our efforts contribute to a more just and equitable world.

4. **Balancing Self-Care and Altruism**: Ethical living requires balancing our own well-being with our commitment to others. We must ensure that we take care of ourselves, so we have the energy and resources to support others effectively.

Real-Life Examples

Many individuals and organizations exemplify the principles of ethical living, demonstrating the positive impact of this approach.

1. **Mahatma Gandhi**: Mahatma Gandhi's life was a testament to ethical living. He championed the principles of nonviolence, justice, and compassion, leading India to independence and inspiring social justice movements worldwide.

2. **The Body Shop**: The Body Shop is a company committed to ethical business practices. They prioritize fair trade, cruelty-free products, and environmental sustainability, demonstrating that businesses can succeed while upholding ethical principles.

3. **Doctors Without Borders**: Doctors Without Borders is an international humanitarian organization that provides medical care to people in crisis. Their work embodies the principles of compassion, justice, and responsibility, addressing urgent health needs and advocating for vulnerable populations.

Conclusion

Ethical living is a journey that requires ongoing reflection, commitment, and action. By balancing our personal well-being with the greater good, we can lead lives of integrity, compassion, and justice. Embracing ethical principles not only enriches our own lives but also contributes to a more harmonious and equitable world. Through mindful decision-making, compassionate action, and advocacy for justice, we can make a positive impact and inspire others to do the same.

Chapter 20

The Art of Self-Discipline: Building Character and Inner Strength

Introduction

Self-discipline is a keystone of personal development, allowing individuals to achieve their goals, nurture inner peace, and maintain ethical standards. Rooted in both ancient wisdom and modern psychology, self-discipline is not merely a trait but a practice that requires commitment, perseverance, and reflection. This chapter explores the essence of self-discipline, its role in building character, and practical strategies for cultivating it in everyday life.

Understanding Self-Discipline

Self-discipline can be defined as the ability to control one's impulses, emotions, and desires to achieve long-term goals. It is the inner strength that allows individuals to act according to their values and priorities, even when faced with challenges or temptations. Unlike external discipline, which is imposed by others, self-discipline arises from within and reflects one's dedication to personal and collective well-being.

The Bhagavad Gita highlights self-discipline as a key virtue for personal growth. Lord Krishna advises Arjuna to act with detachment and focus, emphasizing the importance of self-control and perseverance in the pursuit of dharma (duty). Similarly, modern psychology underscores the role of self-discipline in achieving success and happiness, linking it to traits such as resilience, grit, and emotional intelligence.

The Role of Self-Discipline in Building Character

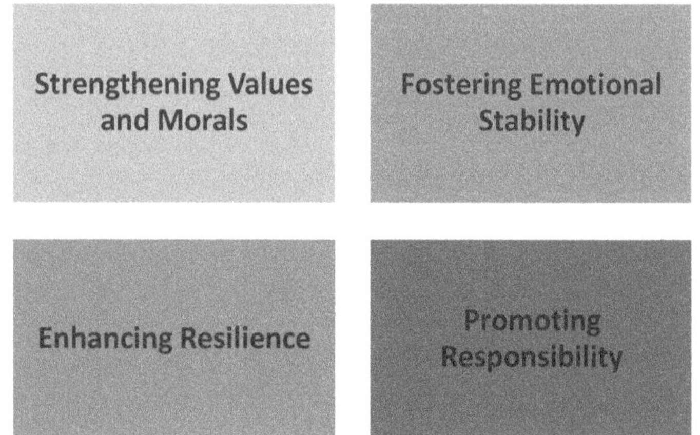

Fig. No. 17 The Role of Self-Discipline in Building Character

1. **Strengthening Values and Morals** Self-discipline aligns actions with values, ensuring consistency between what we believe and how we behave. For instance, practicing honesty and integrity requires the discipline to resist short-term benefits gained through dishonesty. Over time, such disciplined behavior solidifies ethical character.

2. **Fostering Emotional Stability** Emotional regulation is a critical aspect of self-discipline. By managing anger, fear, and anxiety, individuals can respond to situations with calmness and clarity. This stability not only enhances interpersonal relationships but also promotes mental health.

3. **Promoting Responsibility** Self-disciplined individuals take ownership of their actions and decisions. They understand that every choice carries consequences and strive to act responsibly. This sense of accountability builds trust and respect in personal and professional settings.

4. **Enhancing Resilience** Life's challenges often test one's character. Self-discipline equips individuals with the resilience to persevere through hardships and adapt to change. By maintaining focus and determination, they can overcome obstacles and grow stronger in the process.

Cultivating Self-Discipline

1. **Setting Clear Goals** Self-discipline begins with a clear understanding of what one aims to achieve. Define specific, measurable, and meaningful goals that align with your values. Break them down into smaller tasks to make them manageable.

2. **Practicing Mindfulness** Mindfulness helps individuals become aware of their thoughts, emotions, and behaviors. By observing without judgment, one can identify patterns that hinder self-discipline and consciously choose more constructive responses.

3. **Building Healthy Habits** Repetition and consistency are key to developing discipline. Start with small, positive habits—such as waking up early, exercising, or meditating—and gradually expand them. Over time, these habits become part of your routine.

4. **Embracing Delayed Gratification** One of the hallmarks of self-discipline is the ability to prioritize long-term rewards over immediate pleasures. Practice

saying "no" to impulsive desires that conflict with your goals. Techniques like visualization can reinforce the benefits of staying committed.

5. **Learning from Failures** Discipline does not mean perfection. Mistakes are natural and provide valuable lessons. Reflect on setbacks, identify areas for improvement, and recommit to your path with renewed determination.

Self-Discipline and Spiritual Growth

In the spiritual context, self-discipline is essential for self-realization. Practices like yoga, meditation, and pranayama (breath control) require consistent effort and discipline. These practices not only strengthen the mind and body but also deepen one's connection with the inner self.

The concept of tapas (austerity) in Indian philosophy illustrates the transformative power of discipline. Tapas involves enduring discomfort or making sacrifices for a higher purpose. It is seen as a means of purifying the mind and cultivating virtues such as patience, humility, and compassion.

The Rewards of Self-Discipline

1. **Achieving Goals** Self-discipline provides the focus and persistence needed to accomplish personal and professional objectives. By staying committed to your vision, you can turn aspirations into reality.

2. **Boosting Confidence** Each act of self-discipline reinforces a sense of control and mastery. Over time, this builds confidence and self-esteem, empowering you to take on greater challenges.

3. **Nurturing Inner Peace** A disciplined life fosters balance and harmony. By aligning actions with values and managing desires, individuals can experience lasting contentment and inner peace.

Conclusion

Self-discipline is not a one-time effort but a lifelong journey. It requires patience, practice, and a willingness to grow. By embracing self-discipline, you can build a strong character, overcome challenges, and lead a purposeful life. Whether in the pursuit of personal goals, ethical living, or spiritual enlightenment, self-discipline serves as a guiding force that transforms potential into reality.

References

1. Agrawal, M. (2018). *Management* (Latest Edition). Arihant Publications (India) Limited, 403-407.
2. Agarwal, R. (2015). Dharma/Dhamma. In *Religion in Southeast*
3. *Asia: An Encyclopedia of Faiths and Cultures* (pp. 63-66). ABCCLIO. Aristotle. (1999). *Nicomachean ethics* (W. D. Ross, Trans.). Batoche Books. (Original work published ca. 350 B.C.E.)
4. Banks, S. (2009). From professional ethics to ethics in professional life: Implications for learning, teaching and study. *Ethics and Social Welfare, 3*(1), 55-63.
5. Barman, P. (2012). Vivekananda's thoughts on man-making through moral values and character development and its present relevancy in school education. *International Journal of Multidisciplinary Educational Research, 1*(2), 30-37.
6. Basavaraddi, I. (2015). Yoga: Its origin, history and development. Accessed April 23, 2015 through https://mea.gov.in/in-focuS article.htm?25096Yoga+Its+Origin+History+and+De velop ment
7. Bentham, J., & Mill, J. S. (1987). *Utilitarianism and other essays* (A. Ryan, Ed.). Penguin Classics.
8. Brown, M. E., Treviño, L. K., & Harrison, D. A. (2005). Ethical leadership: A social learning perspective for construct development and testing. *Organizational Behavior and Human Decision Processes, 97*(2), 117-134. https://doi.org/10.1016/j.obhdp.2005.03.002
9. Chinmayananda, S. (1996). *The Holy Geeta*. Central Chinmaya Mission Trust.
10. Chouinard, Y., Ellison, J., & Ridgeway, R. (2016). *The responsible company: What we've learned from Patagonia's first 40 years*. Patagonia Books.

11. Ciulla, J. B. (2014). *Ethics, the heart of leadership* (3rd ed.). Praeger. Dalai Lama. (1999). *Ethics for the new millennium.* Riverhead Books.

12. Davidson, R. J., & Begley, S. (2012). *The emotional life of your brain: How its unique patterns affect the way you think, feel, and live— and how you can change them.* Hudson Street Press.

13. Dhulla, T. (2014). A new approach to Indian philosophy and personality- A study. *Indian Journal of Applied Research, 4*(5), 386387.

14. Dutt, P. (2018). The concept of Swadharma and effect on leadership. Accessed August 30, 2018 through https://papers.ssrn.com/sol3/papers.cfm?abstract_id=3205992

15. Easwaran, E. (2007). *The Bhagavad Gita* (2nd ed.). Nilgiri Press. Essays, UK. (2016). Ethics is important to every society philosophy essay. Accessed December 12, 2016 through https://www.ukessays.com/essays/philosophy/ethics-isimportant-to-every-society

16. Essays, UK. (2016). The concept of morality philosophy essay. Accessed December 5, 2016 through https://www.ukessays.com/essays/philosophy/the-conceptof-morality-philosophy-essay.php?vref=1

17. Freeman, R. E., Harrison, J. S., & Wicks, A. C. (2007). *Managing for stakeholders: Survival, reputation, and success.* Yale University Press.

18. Gabriel, R. (2018). Purusharthas: The 4 aims of human life. Accessed May 1, 2018 through https://chopra.com/articles/purushartha-the-aims-ofhuman-life

19. George, B. (2003). *Authentic leadership: Rediscovering the secrets to creating lasting value.* Jossey-Bass.

20. GradesFixer. (2018, October 26). What is karma? Retrieved June 24, 2020, from https://gradesfixer.com/free-essayexamples/what-is-karma/

21. GradesFixer. (2018, December 17). Ethics: How a person should behave in society. Retrieved June 22, 2020, from https://gradesfixer.com/free-essay-example/ethics-how-apersonshould-behave-in-society/

22. Halvac, J. (2017). Professional ethics and professional conduct. *Research Gate*, 70-85.

23. Hawley, J. (2007). *The Bhagavad Gita: A new translation*. Shambhala Publications.

24. Hobbes, T. (1651). *Leviathan*. Oxford University Press.

25. Hurst, K. (n.d.). The 12 spiritual laws of the universe and what they mean. Accessed through https://www.thelawofattraction.com/12-spiritual-lawsuniverse/

26. Iyer, N. (2013). The four goals of life. *Speaking Tree.in*. Accessed December 14, 2013 through https://www.speakingtree.in/blog/the-four-goals-oflife/mlite#aoh=15929839489724&referrer=https%3A%2F%2Fwww.google.com

27. Jha, B. (2015). A critical study about the Nyaya theory of prama and pramanas. *Journal of Humanities and Social Sciences, 20*(11), 30-32.

28. Johnson, C. E. (2018). *Meeting the ethical challenges of leadership: Casting light or shadow* (6th ed.). SAGE Publications.

29. Johnson & Johnson. (2022). Our Credo. Retrieved from https://www.jnj.com/credo/

30. Kabat-Zinn, J. (2013). *Full catastrophe living: Using the wisdom of your body and mind to face stress, pain, and illness* (Revised and updated edition). Bantam Books.

31. Kant, I. (1993). *Grounding for the metaphysics of morals* (J. W. Ellington, Trans.). Hackett Publishing Company. (Original work published 1785)

32. Kaur, M. (2017). Effect of yoga and meditation on stress management of female prisoners in Delhi– A review

paper. *International Journal of Science Technology and Management, 5*(12), 494-499.

33. Kaur, N. (2005). *Sikhism: An introduction*. I.B. Tauris.

34. Kohlberg's theory of moral development. (2019). Accessed September 28, 2019 through https://www.verywellmind.com/kohlbergs-theory-of-moraldevelopment-2795071

35. Kouzes, J. M., & Posner, B. Z. (2017). *The leadership challenge: How to make extraordinary things happen in organizations* (6th ed.). Jossey-Bass.

36. Krentzman, A. What is spirituality. Accessed through https://www.takingcharge.csh.umn.edu/what-spirituality Lal, V. (2017). Human values in educational institutions. *Global Journal for Research Analysis, 6*(9), 77-78.

37. MacIntyre, A. (2007). *After virtue: A study in moral theory* (3rd ed.). University of Notre Dame Press.

38. McCarney, J. (1970). *The concept of morality* (PhD Thesis). University of Warwick.

39. McLeod, S. A. (2013, October 24). Kohlberg's stages of moral development. *Simply Psychology*. Accessed through https://www.simplypsychology.org/kohlberg.html

40. Mintz, S. (2018). What are values. Accessed August 08, 2018 through https://www.ethicssage.com/2018/08/what-arevalues.html

41. Mohita, N. (n.d.). Ethics of philosophy by M. K. Gandhi: Notes on Satya, Ahimsa, ends and means. Accessed through https://www.yourarticlelibrary.com/philosophy/ethics-ofphilosophy-by-m-k-gandhi-notes-on-satya-ahimsa-ends-andmeans/10164

42. Murty, R. (n.d.). Ashrama system in Puranas. *Indian Culture*, 28.

43. Naomi, et al. (2018). The psychology of morality: A review and analysis of empirical studies published from

1940 through 2017. *SAGE Journals.* https://doi.org/10.1177/1088868318811759

44. Neff, K. D. (2011). *Self-compassion: The proven power of being kind to yourself.* William Morrow.

45. Niekerk, B. (2018). Religion and spirituality: What are the fundamental differences? *HTS Teologiese Studies/Theological Studies*, 1-11.

46. Nhat Hanh, T. (1991). *Peace is every step: The path of mindfulness in everyday life.* Bantam Books.

47. Patagonia. (n.d.). Environmental & social responsibility. Retrieved from https://www.patagonia.com/environmentalresponsibility/

48. Raina, K. (2016). The levels of human consciousness and creative functioning: Insights from the theory of Pancha Kosha (Five Sheaths of Consciousness). *Vol. 48*(2), 168-189. Rastogi, K. (2019). Exploring Swadharma. *The International Journal of Indian Psychology, 6*(3), 27-29.

49. Ratnawat, R. G. (2018). Understanding values and their role in human life. Accessed May 31, 2018 through

50. https://www.hrkatha.com/opinion/understanding-valuesand-their-role-in-human-life/

51. Rich, L. (n.d.). Introduction to ethics. *Jones & Bartlett Learning*, 3-30.

52. Roy, S. (2020). Different types of pramanas. Accessed April 21, 2020 through https://ugcnetpaper1.com/different-typesof-pramans

53. Kumar, A. (2013). *The spiritual roots of yoga: Unlocking the ancient wisdom of Patanjali.* New World Library.

54. Ryan, R. M., & Deci, E. L. (2000). Self-determination theory and the facilitation of intrinsic motivation, social development, and well-being. *American Psychologist, 55*(1), 68–78.